AMERICAN
SOCIAL
MOVEMENTS

THE ANTIWAR
MOVEMENT

Randy Scherer, *Book Editor*

Bruce Glassman, *Vice President*
Bonnie Szumski, *Publisher*
Scott Barbour, *Managing Editor*

**GREENHAVEN
PRESS ®**

THOMSON
——————✦——————™
GALE

San Diego • Detroit • New York • San Francisco • Cleveland
New Haven, Conn. • Waterville, Maine • London • Munich

For more information, contact
Greenhaven Press
27500 Drake Rd.
Farmington Hills, MI 48331-3535
Or you can visit our Internet site at http://www.gale.com

LIBRARY OF CONGRESS CATALOGING-IN-PUBLICATION DATA

The antiwar movement / Randy Scherer, book editor.
   p. cm. — (American social movements)
  Includes bibliographical references and index.
  ISBN 0-7377-1944-3 (pbk. : alk. paper) — ISBN 0-7377-1943-5 (lib. : alk. paper)
    1. Peace movements—United States—History. 2. Pacifists—United States—History. I. Scherer, Randy. II. Series.
  JZ5584.U55A58 2004
  303.6'6'0973—dc22   2003059934

Printed in the United States of America

CONTENTS

The government reacted by enacting laws to quell dissent and limit people's right to free speech.

Chapter 3 • THE 1960S AND THE VIETNAM WAR

took a stand in favor of the public's right to know the actions of its government by publishing the U.S. government's secret history of the Vietnam War. This report of the secret history is known as the Pentagon Papers.

The widespread antiwar protests of the 1960s had many successes and failures. However, public opinion and antiwar protesters influenced political leaders more than members of the antiwar movement understood at the time.

Chapter 4 • ISSUES CONFRONTING THE ANTIWAR MOVEMENT

In order to rid the world of terrorists, the United States must renounce war and instead focus on a peaceful strategy of cooperation and compassion.

The Founding Fathers laid the groundwork for a strong antiwar movement in their ideals of democracy, justice, and equality. By adhering to these ideals, the antiwar movement will increase its success.

Although antiwar protests did not stop the 2003 war in Iraq, this setback is not a failure for the antiwar movement. The antiwar movement needs to focus on its goal of global disarmament, multilateral diplomacy, and electing a new leadership to the White House.

Western culture's belief that war is justifiable has marginalized philosophies of pacifism and has encouraged leaders to reject peaceful responses to conflict.

Chapter 5 • VOICES FOR PEACE: WORLD PERSPECTIVES

FOREWORD

Historians Gary T. Marx and Douglas McAdam define a social movement as "organized efforts to promote or resist change in society that rely, at least in part, on noninstitutionalized forms of political action." Examining American social movements broadens and vitalizes the study of history by allowing students to observe the efforts of ordinary individuals and groups to oppose the established values of their era, often in unconventional ways. The civil rights movement of the twentieth century, for example, began as an effort to challenge legalized racial segregation and garner social and political rights for African Americans. Several grassroots organizations—groups of ordinary citizens committed to social activism—came together to organize boycotts, sit-ins, voter registration drives, and demonstrations to counteract racial discrimination. Initially, the movement faced massive opposition from white citizens, who had long been accustomed to the social standards that required the separation of the races in almost all areas of life. But the movement's consistent use of an innovative form of protest—nonviolent direct action—eventually aroused the public conscience, which in turn paved the way for major legislative victories such as the Civil Rights Act of 1964 and the Voting Rights Act of 1965. Examining the civil rights movement reveals how ordinary people can use nonstandard political strategies to change society.

Investigating the style, tactics, personalities, and ideologies of American social movements also encourages students to learn about aspects of history and culture that may receive scant attention in textbooks. As scholar Eric Foner notes, American history "has been constructed not only in congressional debates and political treatises, but also on plantations and picket lines, in parlors and bedrooms. Frederick Douglass, Eugene V. Debs, and Margaret Sanger . . . are its architects as well as Thomas Jefferson and Abraham Lincoln." While not all

American social movements garner popular support or lead to epoch-changing legislation, they each offer their own unique insight into a young democracy's political dialogue.

Each book in Greenhaven's American Social Movements series allows readers to follow the general progression of a particular social movement—examining its historical roots and beginnings in earlier chapters and relatively recent and contemporary information (or even the movement's demise) in later chapters. With the incorporation of both primary and secondary sources, as well as writings by both supporters and critics of the movement, each anthology provides an engaging panoramic view of its subject. Selections include a variety of readings, such as book excerpts, newspaper articles, speeches, manifestos, literary essays, interviews, and personal narratives. The editors of each volume aim to include the voices of movement leaders and participants as well as the opinions of historians, social analysts, and individuals who have been affected by the movement. This comprehensive approach gives students the opportunity to view these movements both as participants have experienced them and as historians and critics have interpreted them.

Every volume in the American Social Movements series includes an introductory essay that presents a broad historical overview of the movement in question. The annotated table of contents and comprehensive index help readers quickly locate material of interest. Each selection is preceded by an introductory paragraph that summarizes the article's content and provides historical context when necessary. Several other research aids are also present, including brief excerpts of supplementary material, a chronology of major events pertaining to the movement, and an accessible bibliography.

The Greenhaven Press American Social Movements series offers readers an informative introduction to some of the most fascinating groups and ideas in American history. The contents of each anthology provide a valuable resource for general readers as well as for enthusiasts of American political science, history, and culture.

INTRODUCTION

W hen thinking of the term *antiwar*, it is tempting to look back through American history and identify individual movements against specific wars—the Vietnam era protests of the 1960s and 1970s, the anti-imperialist movement at the turn of the twentieth century, or the most recent protests against the 2003 war in Iraq. However, these antiwar movements were actually temporary manifestations of a broad movement for a peaceful and just society in which war and violence are viewed as ineffective methods for conflict resolution.

Many of the movement's leaders do not consider *antiwar* to be an applicable term, as the absence of war is only one aspect of a much broader worldview. In fact, the term *peace movement* may be more appropriate, because the movement's goal is the creation of a just and sustainable society in which many of the present-day, large-scale causes of violence and instability are removed or mitigated. These causes include unjust political situations, illegitimate or authoritarian political leaders, unsustainable consumption, population growth, poverty, racism, and poor education. For the purposes of this book, however, the discussion of the antiwar movement will focus specifically on the actions of the peace movement to minimize or eliminate war—as a result, the term *antiwar* will be used.

Because militarism is such an ingrained part of the West's, indeed the world's, behavior, leaders of the antiwar movement are aware that they fight an uphill battle. Hamline University philosophy professor Duane Cady speaks for many in the antiwar movement when he states that Western culture's belief that war is justifiable has marginalized philosophies of pacifism. Cady writes that the actual definition of the term *peace* has been altered in American culture to simply mean an absence of war. As a result, peaceful solutions to large-scale conflict are only entertained for a short time. Peaceful solutions can be time-consuming, involve challenging rounds of negotiation and diplomacy, and often require compromise. Violent solutions are often viewed as more "realistic" because war is a life-and-death endeavor that forces everyone involved to take one of two sides. As a result, the use of war as a method of conflict resolution is usually considered more desirable by politicians and military leaders weighing their options.

HAWKS AND DOVES

American political leaders often take one of two positions on conflict resolution—they become what is popularly known as either *hawks* or *doves*. Hawks tend to favor military solutions, while doves focus on peaceful solutions to a wide variety of problems. Negotiations, diplomacy, and economic sanctions are the common methods cited by antiwar leaders as legitimate ways to advance American interests. At the same time, the antiwar movement seeks to eliminate the causes of war described above. In seeking solutions to these worldwide, multifaceted problems, therefore, the doves try to avert warfare before it can begin.

Furthermore, doves tend to favor multinational coalitions that try to create solutions to large-scale problems. Organizations such as the United Nations (UN), the North Atlantic Treaty Organzation (NATO), the European Union (EU), and the International Court of Justice are viewed as legitimate governing bodies that encourage world peace. Interestingly, when these organizations support warfare, such as during the 1991 Gulf War, many liberal or moderate antiwar leaders tend to agree.

Hawks and doves repeatedly face off for power within the American government. One ongoing struggle involves a think tank called Project for the New American Century (PNAC), which advocates the use of American military power to expand the "American empire" in order to exert influence over the world. President George W. Bush's administration has close ties to PNAC. Vice President Dick Cheney, Secretary of Defense Donald Rumsfeld, and President Bush's brother, Florida governor Jeb Bush, are among the signatories of PNAC's Statement of Principles. Other notable members are Department of Defense leaders Richard Armitage, Richard Perle, and Paul Wolfowitz. For most of Bush's tenure in office, antiwar leaders have complained that doves have been forced out of the loop and made incapable of influencing policy.

THE BENEFITS OF WAR

Beginning in the late nineteenth century, American antiwar groups began to critically consider the reasons that political and economic leaders may support war. The groups concluded that the true purpose of using warfare as a means to resolve conflict was threefold—to squelch domestic dissent, to provide for personal advancement, and to afford businesses the opportunity to expand and increase their profits.

The antiwar movement argues that one of the main reasons leaders choose war is that it has the power to deflect whatever internal domestic anger may exist within a nation onto an external enemy. Put another way, war convinces disillusioned citizens to stand behind their government and vent their frustrations on a third, external party. Frequently, this phenomenon involves the lower and middle classes, who are often troubled by such domestic shortcomings as joblessness, lack of health care, poor education, political disenfranchisement, and dissatisfaction with particular politicians. These shortcomings can be minimized and even eliminated during wartime by focusing attention on an outside "enemy." To this end, politicians, business leaders, and military leaders commonly argue that the only concern during wartime should be how to best support the troops. Antiwar leaders feel that this singular focus during wartime is inconsistent with American values of free speech, the right to petition the government, and the expectation that government decisions are ultimately open to public scrutiny.

Second, warfare allows for significant personal advancement. It offers many individuals the chance to display their loyalty and courage by joining the military, which in turn can provide educational or vocational training (often at little to no personal financial cost). Such patriotism often raises a person's status within American culture. Many members of the lower classes and of minority groups have knowingly looked past the fact that they disproportionately pay the costs of war (in death, disfigurement, disease, mental anguish, etc.) in order to gain the chance to prove their loyalty or improve their socioeconomic status.

Thirdly, warfare can be good for business. Throughout American history, major U.S. corporations and other forms of big business have almost unanimously supported warfare as a means of resolving international conflicts—most likely because war is often a tool used to gain access to foreign markets and thus fosters American business. Wartime also creates a demand for huge amounts of military matériel often produced by American manufacturers, and postwar reconstruction contracts can be worth enormous amounts of money.

It was with all of these benefits in mind that President Theodore Roosevelt wrote to a friend in 1897, "In strict confidence . . . I should welcome almost any war, for I think this country needs one." When Roosevelt made this statement, there was growing consensus among America's leaders that warfare must be used to unify disgruntled workers, expand America's economic markets, and secure political and economic power for the upper classes. Beginning in the late 1800s, critics of this path had been quick to point out that at least one, if not all three, of the aforementioned attributes of warfare has been the primary motivation for abandoning peaceful means of conflict resolution in almost all of America's foreign wars. According to the antiwar movement, the truth is not that peaceful resolution is inadequate, but that warfare can be more immediately profitable.

The antiwar movement continues to argue that these "benefits" are the main motivators for the use of warfare as an instrument of foreign policy. The movement also maintains that warfare has rarely solved any of the problems that it claims to repair. It merely offers a temporary fix that is attractive to the upper classes of American society—many of whom never have to face the horrors of war and only enjoy its benefits.

Antiwar leaders admit that peaceful means, such as negotiations, diplomacy, and sanctions, may take longer or seem less decisive than warfare, but they insist that in the vast majority of situations, nonviolent methods of conflict resolution are superior to warfare.

THE DOCTRINE OF THE JUST WAR

The American antiwar movement has its philosophical roots in the many small religious groups that gathered on both sides of the Atlantic during the seventeenth and eighteenth centuries. Forming the earliest antiwar movement, these groups saw a contradiction between the policies of war that were advanced by their kings and the teachings of the Bible.

Functioning as a basic set of "rules," the catechism of the Catholic Church explains the teachings and principles of Jesus Christ, as well as the many religious leaders who developed Christian thought. A portion of the catechism sets guidelines for the appropriate use of force by any nation. The catechism lays down the idea of "just war," which is war undertaken for noble, justifiable reasons and guided by humanistic rules. The doctrine of the just war states that all of the rules must be completely satisfied in order for a war to be truly just.

The doctrine begins by quoting the famous commandment "thou shalt not kill" and continues with the statement that "anger is a desire for revenge." In this way it firmly establishes that war may be undertaken only for self-defense against an aggressor that has inflicted "lasting, grave and certain" damage. All other means of dealing with the aggressor must be attempted and have to have failed in order for war to be an option. Furthermore, there must be serious prospects for success. Importantly, the use of force must not create evils greater than those that are to be eliminated—including the destruction of entire cities or other forms of wholesale, indiscriminate violence. The just war doctrine also stipulates that special consideration must be taken for noncombatants, or civilians; thus it seeks to minimize harm to as many people as possible. To this end, the catechism states that all acts of war must be consistent

with proper morals and that blind allegiance is unacceptable—
all parties involved must continue to use their own powers of
judgment and always do what they know to be right. By the
mid–twentieth century, the principles of the just war doctrine
had become incorporated into international law.

The doctrine of the just war has played a key role in the debates surrounding almost all American wars. During every foreign war in American history, both government leaders and
members of the antiwar movement have argued their case either for or against war based on its principles. The prowar
leaders have repeatedly stated that they adhere to the doctrine
of the just war, going to war only in self-defense and only
when all other means of resolving the conflict have failed.
They also insist that the United States does not target civilians.
The antiwar movement, on the other hand, has repeatedly
stated that the prowar leaders have not given peaceful means
appropriate consideration. They also charge that noncombatants are unjustly harmed or killed as a result of warfare.

The American-led 2003 war in Iraq is a good example of
how both hawks and doves cite the doctrine of the just war.
President George W. Bush, a known hawk, repeatedly stated
that the suspected possession of weapons of mass destruction
by the Iraqi government was a threat to America; that all other
means of dealing with Iraqi dictator Saddam Hussein had been
exhausted; and that military strikes would be limited to military targets with full efforts made to spare Iraqi civilians. Bush
insisted that force was a justifiable method for dealing with this
problem. Although Iraq had not taken direct action against the
United States, Bush said that the nation could not wait for this
to happen and must preemptively remove the perceived threat.

However, doves do not feel that Bush was accurate in his
justification for war or in his assessment of the war's impact
on the region. In fact, many antiwar leaders state that all cate-
gories of the just war doctrine were violated by the Bush administration's invasion of Iraq. Antiwar leaders cite the fact that
no evidence of weapons of mass destruction was uncovered
as proof that the previous decade of inspections and economic

sanctions had worked and that the war was unnecessary. Furthermore, antiwar leaders refute the claim that damage to civilians was minimized. They say that the use of depleted-uranium munitions by American soldiers causes cancer, birth defects, and many other dangerous effects for many years on all people in the areas in which the munitions are used—which is everywhere that shots are fired in modern war. As evidenced by this most recent conflict, the just war doctrine continues to guide modern nations in military undertakings, although it is often a source of debate.

CIVIL DISOBEDIENCE AND THE ANTIWAR MOVEMENT

Another important root of the American antiwar movement is civil disobedience, which is typically understood as the will ful violation of laws in order to draw attention to a cause or to change the actions of the government. In the late 1800s, American author Henry David Thoreau developed the concept of civil disobedience, providing many of America's future social leaders, including the leaders of the antiwar movement, the civil rights movement, and the feminist movement, with a primary tactic for advancing their cause. In 1864, Thoreau refused to pay taxes that would support the Mexican War and slavery—both undertakings by the U.S. government that Thoreau did not support. Thoreau stated that governments derive their power from the actions of the common people and that the surest way to change the government's actions is to eliminate economic support. Just as one could force a private company to change its actions by not purchasing its products, so too can civilians impress their ideas upon the government by denying it funding, blocking access to buildings, or organizing other large-scale demonstrations that interrupt the normal flow of daily life.

Thoreau's concept of civil disobedience was a direct influence on Mahatma Gandhi and Martin Luther King Jr., two of the most successful leaders of peaceful social movements in history. Using tactics of civil disobedience, in 1947 Gandhi led

India to independence from British colonial rule. Although Indian independence did not occur without violence, Gandhi's example of nonviolent resistance was an inspiration to people worldwide, including the antiwar movement.

Martin Luther King Jr. was a leader of the civil rights movement in America who fought for equal rights for all citizens from the mid-1950s until his death in 1968. By the late 1960s, King was working to tie together the civil rights movement and the antiwar movement, seeing them as two versions of the same desire for a peaceful, just society. Using tactics that were borrowed directly from both Thoreau and Gandhi, King helped achieve equal rights under the law for ethnic and racial minorities in only a decade—a feat that had not been properly accomplished in the 150 years of American history prior to King's entry into the political world.

More than 140 years after Thoreau's death, his doctrine of civil disobedience is still commonly practiced in the form of boycotts, strikes, protests, refusal to pay taxes, and refusal to perform military service. From year to year, president to president, and war to war, the antiwar movement revisits similar tactics of civil disobedience to advance its nonviolent agenda.

ANTI-IMPERIALISTS

In addition to the catechism of the Catholic Church and the concept of civil disobedience, the philosophy of anti-imperialism serves as a third root of the antiwar movement. Imperialism is generally regarded as a policy of extending a nation's authority over other nations by territorial, economic, or political domination. Anti-imperialism rejects these methods.

By the late 1800s, many U.S. businesses were expanding beyond America's borders in pursuit of untapped markets for American goods as well as unmined resources for American companies. In the wake of these expansions, an ideological debate emerged in the 1890s. Imperialists such as President Theodore Roosevelt and Senator Henry Cabot Lodge advocated military conquest of whatever lands, resources, and markets that America desired. Another corner in the debate was represented by business leaders, who advocated a more subtle approach to imperialism known as the "open door" policy, in which American businesses would lead the charge overseas, and the military would be used only against foreign countries that opposed America's expansion. Anti-imperialists, on the other hand, such as politician William Jennings Bryan and author Mark Twain, promoted two alternatives for enriching America. One was a system in which internal wealth would be used improve conditions for America's lower classes before the upper classes were allowed to increase their own fortunes. The second alternative stressed working with many foreign nations for mutual benefits.

Anti-imperialist ideology centered on the principle that America should not mimic the self-destructive behavior of "old-world" empires, such as Great Britain or ancient Rome. Many of these empires failed because they repeated specific, large-scale errors, including the overextension of the military, entry into costly, far-off wars, and attempts to control far-flung territories with no concern for, or assistance from, other nations. These empires were also criticized for conquering weaker, less organized nations in the pursuit of natural resources or treasures. Anti-imperialists argued that imperialistic desires have no long-term benefits and eventually lead to the failure of the empire, causing it to shrink to a less powerful position. Instead, anti-imperialists favor the independence of each nation and the development of sustainable ties between successful sovereign states.

Over time, this ideology has become central to the antiwar movement. Anti-imperialism is visible in the arguments against almost all of America's foreign wars, with the exception of World War II. The Spanish-American War and the subsequent Philippine War at the end of the 1800s saw the birth of a formal anti-imperialist philosophy. World War I, the Vietnam War, and the 2003 war in Iraq were particular targets for the anti-imperialists because these wars centered on the acquisition of power and influence for the United States and seemed to have little to do with self-defense, in the eyes of antiwar leaders.

WORLD WAR I

World War I saw the emergence of an adversarial relationship between the antiwar movement and the U.S. government that remains to the present day. The movement for peace began to clash with the U.S. government as each competed for influence over the minds of everyday citizens. As the antiwar movement grew in popularity during the early twentieth century, the government began to develop methods to eliminate this competition.

In the beginning of the twentieth century, the lower and middle classes began to organize small social movements to improve the terrible conditions of workers in mines and factories. During this time, men, women, and children routinely worked eighty hours a week, weekends included, in incredibly difficult and dangerous jobs. Few laws protected them and even fewer politicians seemed to look out for their interests. The general attitude of most of the working class was that the richest Americans enjoyed far greater benefits than all of the other classes and that they used those benefits to maintain their elevated status. Strikes and protests became commonplace, and millions of workers joined unions, hoping to make business leaders hear their concerns.

Amid these developments, socialism was growing in the United States. Socialism is a political ideology that advocates the good of the collective over the good of the individual. Promising to lift the lower classes to better positions in American society, socialist politicians were gaining respect and power. In the early twentieth century, the Socialist Party had one hundred thousand registered members and twelve hundred public officeholders across the country. Its leader, Eugene V. Debs, ran for president five times; at the peak of his popularity, he garnered over nine hundred thousand votes.

When World War I began, many Americans voiced concerns that America was entering a foreign war to gain power, influence, and access to overseas markets. The socialist message centered on the idea that the elites within America's government, military, and corporations were using the lower classes to work in the factories and would now use them to fight a war from which they would not benefit.

Initially, President Woodrow Wilson declared that America would remain neutral in the war, stating "there is such a thing as a nation too proud to fight." However, America quickly began to ship military supplies to its Allies involved in the war, using civilian ships with falsified records to slip materials past the German navy. When Germany sank the *Lusitania* (a British vessel being used for such purposes), Wilson claimed that the Germans had engaged in an unprovoked attack on American citizens. In truth, the *Lusitania* was en route to England to deliver almost seven thousand crates of ammunition under a phony manifest, using unaware civilians as a shield.

The sinking of the *Lusitania*, along with other diplomatic crises, led the United States to enter the war on the side of the Allies in April 1917. Antiwar leaders, such as Debs and anarchist Emma Goldman, objected, stating that the American leadership was guiding the public toward an imperialistic war that would benefit only the upper classes. Despite President Wilson's promises that World War I would be "a war to end all wars," the American public did not get behind the war with any degree of enthusiasm. One million troops were needed, but in the six weeks following the U.S. entry into the war, only seventy-three thousand volunteered. Congress quickly instituted a draft to raise the necessary troops.

With the draft, Congress also passed the Espionage Act. Although the name of the act implied that it was aimed at foreign spies within the United States, the Espionage Act was primarily used to control domestic dissent. Under the auspices of the Espionage Act, prosecutors and police targeted antiwar leaders, particularly among the Socialist Party, because their message was critical of the government and thus seen as subversive. The Espionage Act was immediately criticized by the antiwar movement and others as unconstitutional, but in an interesting twist, those who criticized the act were imprisoned under it.

Through the use of the Espionage Act, the U.S. government argued that simply criticizing the war could hamper the ability of the government to raise the necessary troops. Therefore, speaking against the war, distributing antiwar pamphlets, or otherwise advertising that the war was unjust could be interpreted as aiding the enemy. Although criticized as a direct contradiction of the First Amendment and American values, this argument was successfully used to imprison hundreds of antiwar protesters. Among the leaders imprisoned was Eugene Debs, who was sentenced to ten years in prison for publicly stating that the Espionage Act was unconstitutional.

By the end of World War I, the United States had virtually eliminated all political competition to the two major parties through the use of the Espionage Act. It had also imprisoned or deported almost all significant antiwar leaders. Moreover, through these experiences, U.S. politicians learned a valuable lesson in their fight against the continuing antiwar movement. They learned that simply speaking against any American war effort could be interpreted as damaging to the U.S. military and as supporting the enemy—and that the public and even the Supreme Court would agree with this argument.

THE ANTIWAR MOVEMENT FROM WORLD WAR II TO VIETNAM

Although the antiwar movement was extremely strong in America at the start of World War I, by the Great War's end the Espionage Act had forced it almost entirely underground. As more and more antiwar leaders were imprisoned, the antiwar movement came to be regarded as treasonous and heretical to American values. At this critical time the antiwar movement suffered what seemed to be its final defeat—the onset of World War II. As Nazi leader Adolf Hitler marched across Europe, the European leaders made the fatal mistake of trying to appease him, hoping that if Hitler were given some land and power, he would stop his continental conquest. This strategy was a failure, however, and only caused Hitler to grow bolder and more powerful. Even though few antiwar leaders supported the policy of appeasement at the time, the movement became linked with the appeasement approach, making future arguments against military action seem weak.

However, the antiwar movement drew some strength in the wake of the firebombing of Dresden, Germany, and the dropping of atomic bombs on Hiroshima and Nagasaki, Japan, in 1945. In the case of Dresden, the United States destroyed a city that had almost no involvement in the war and was primarily a place of art, music, and culture. At the time of the bombing, it was almost entirely populated by women, children, the elderly, and prisoners of war. Similarly, when atomic bombs were dropped on Hiroshima and Nagasaki, World War II was arguably all but over and the bombings were not absolutely necessary to declare victory. The wholesale destruction caused by these three incidents shocked the world. Three major cities were completely destroyed, and millions of people were killed and sickened from only a few days of bombing. The world community immediately recognized that many modern weapons were simply too powerful to have a productive use. Led by renowned scientist Albert Einstein and philosopher and social critic Bertrand Russell, many nations came together to outlaw the use of such weapons.

However, this victory was short-lived. The Cold War that followed World War II featured an arms race with the Soviet Union, as well as many small clashes and proxy wars in the battle between Western democracy and communism. Citizens or groups that advocated nonmilitary solutions during this period faced charges similar to those leveled under the Espionage Act—that any criticism of U.S. policy is actually support for the enemy. Senator Joseph McCarthy took this line of reasoning to an extreme, claiming that Communists had infiltrated the United States and were actively seeking to undermine its ability to win the Cold War. McCarthy even claimed that Communists had infiltrated the State Department and Congress. Although this attitude may seem paranoid or farfetched, the fear of Communists affected every aspect of American politics. The Senate and House of Representatives held many hearings to determine if prominent citizens or politicians were actually Communists in disguise, although no Communists were found. Because McCarthyists saw antiwar protesters as sympathetic to communism, the antiwar movement was kept on the defensive for many years.

As the Cold War continued and the arms race mounted, antiwar tactics finally made their way into the mainstream political arena and became useful ways to handle major international problems. Always stressing negotiations and diplomacy, the antiwar movement enjoyed its first public victory in years with President John F. Kennedy's handling of the Cuban missile crisis. In 1962, it was discovered that the Soviet Union had deployed nuclear missiles in Cuba, within striking distance of the United States. Many Americans feared that nuclear war was inevitable. However, Kennedy stuck to peaceful means and successfully negotiated a solution that not only ended the crisis, but also benefited the United States in the long run. Antiwar leaders and the American public celebrated, as a potential nuclear war was averted and diplomacy triumphed over violence.

In the 1960s, the antiwar movement continued to gain support from American citizens. As the United States increased its involvement in the ongoing Vietnam War (the French had already been fighting in Indochina for decades), the antiwar movement slowly attracted more people, taking on an increasingly larger role in the daily life of Americans. The teachings of leaders such as Mahatma Gandhi and Martin Luther King Jr. came to the forefront, and the civil rights movement became tied to the antiwar movement—natural partners, as each aimed to guide the world toward a peaceful, just, and sustainable existence.

The gaining momentum of the antiwar movement put pressure on the U.S. government during this time, however. To counter the growing movement, FBI director J. Edgar Hoover launched a counterintelligence program known as Cointelpro. Cointelpro was a secret, illegal program to identify and "neutralize" any form of dissent against established government policies. It was aimed at many of America's activist leaders, including King, and sought to infiltrate their organizations and disrupt their ability to function. Cointelpro was sustained from the mid-1960s through 1972, when it was exposed and the FBI quickly terminated it. During that time, over 1 million Americans were the subjects of illegal surveillance and harassment. After the collapse of the Soviet Union and the end of the Cold War, the antiwar movement continued to oppose injustice, poverty, and violence around the world. By the beginning of the twenty-first century, antiwar leaders had access to a powerful new tool—the Internet. Over the Internet, antiwar leaders immediately began to advocate a peaceful response to the September 11, 2001, terrorist attacks on the World Trade Center and the Pentagon. Groups including relatives of those killed in the attacks, prominent social leaders, and ordinary American citizens used the Internet to spread their antiwar message and to organize for coming debates with prowar politicians.

Immediately after September 11, 2001, families of some of the victims of the terrorist attacks organized a group known as Not in Our Name. This group advocated a peaceful handling of the attacks, arguing that a militaristic response would only create further violence for years to come. However, American public opinion overwhelmingly supported military action to capture Osama bin Laden, the terrorist leader suspected of masterminding the attacks. In addition, the U.S. military enjoyed support from most foreign nations and international organizations, as well as from many moderate or liberal antiwar groups, since many saw the hunt for bin Laden as a just military operation. As a result, the hard-line antiwar leaders were temporarily moved to the background of the debate.

Less than two years later, the antiwar movement was again drawn to the center of American public policy when the Bush administration began gathering support for a military invasion of Iraq. On February 15 and 16, 2003, antiwar leaders used the Internet to organize the single largest demonstration in history, bringing together an estimated 10 million protesters in every state in the United States and hundreds of cities around the world. The New York Times called the antiwar leaders and demonstrators "the other superpower." Although these demonstrations did not prevent the war, the massive display of opposition injected the movement with a dose of optimism and proved to the nation and the world that America did not speak with just one voice.

The work of the antiwar movement is arduous, its fight ongoing; in the grand scheme of international events, its mission can seem at times fraught with disappointment. However, its contribution to American politics and the world order has been vital, even if subtle, and many of its victories may occur in secret, unknown even to antiwar supporters themselves. One example of this phenomenon is President Eisenhower's decision to refrain from using nuclear weapons against China during the early years of the Cold War. In the mid-1950s, the pacifist organization known as the Fellowship of Reconciliation learned of a famine in China and launched a campaign in which members mailed thousands of little bags of rice to the White House. Attached to the bags was a quotation from the Bible: "If thine enemy hunger, feed him." For many years, the campaign was considered a failure. The president never publicly acknowledged receiving the bags of rice, and certainly none were sent to China. However, it was later learned that the campaign played a significant, perhaps even a determining, role in preventing war between the United States and China. When President Eisenhower met with his advisers to contemplate U.S. options in the conflict, his generals twice advised him to consider using nuclear weapons. Eisenhower reportedly turned to his aides and asked how many little bags of rice had come in. Upon hearing they numbered in the tens of thousands, the president told his generals that as long as so many Americans supported feeding the Chinese instead of bombing them, he could not consider using nuclear weapons against them.

It is these private and modest successes that embolden the antiwar movement and sustain it from generation to generation. Leaders of the antiwar movement remain hopeful that through effective communication and large-scale organization, they can create a more peaceful international order.

CHAPTER 1

ROOTS OF THE ANTIWAR MOVEMENT

AMERICAN
SOCIAL
MOVEMENTS

A History of
Pacifism in
Colonial Europe
and Early America

CHARLES CHATFIELD AND RUZANNA ILUKHINA

In the following selection, American historian Charles Chatfield and Russian historian Ruzanna Ilukhina describe the history of the social and political trends that shaped antiwar movements in colonial Europe and early America. They explore the philosophical roots of pacifism in the writings of political thinkers such as Niccolò Machiavelli, Jean-Jacques Rousseau, and Immanuel Kant. The authors also discuss the development of citizen groups that began to organize in the United States and England to oppose war beginning in the early 1800s.

A professor of history at Wittenberg University in Ohio, Charles Chatfield has published ten books and has worked with many of America's leading historians. However, he cites this collaboration with Ilukhina, which was unprecedented due to the Cold War, as his most interesting scholarly experience. Ruzanna Ilukhina is a history professor at the Institute of General History at the Russian Academy of Science and has traveled throughout the world as both a historian and peace activist.

The just war tradition asserted that peace (in the sense of order) is realistic only as a set of criteria that limit warfare, which, it assumed, is a necessary condition of society. Virtually all attempts to restrict warfare were made by the dominant classes. In the midst of the widespread violence of the thirteenth and fourteenth centuries, however, there were spontaneous, popular movements for peace in the form of mass devotionals, processions, and demonstrations: perhaps 400,000 people converged on Verona one day in 1233, perhaps 200,000 on Rome in September 1399. These crowds were not asking for a mere limitation of warfare; they were appealing for an end to it. Such movements were the precursors of peace advocacy.

By the sixteenth century, the feudal and Catholic structure of western Europe was being supplanted by the development of modern nation-states, along with capitalism and Protestant religions. The century was marked by a breathtaking surge of spiritual culture, art, and science, but it was also an epoch of bloody and almost incessant warfare that culminated in the devastating Thirty Years War (1618–1648), while the shadow of the Turkish empire posed a threat that preoccupied the rulers of the region. The way was open for modern peace advocacy.

The advocacy of peace was heralded by outcries against violence and by appeals for an end to destructiveness and irrationality. The preeminent voice was that of Desiderius Erasmus of Rotterdam. The recognized leader of European humanists, Erasmus condemned war most eloquently in his classic *Complaint of Peace* and in his shorter, more urbane reflections on adages, or proverbs. He insisted that human nature is ordained for peace and not war, and that a ruler's legitimacy comes not from power itself, but rather from the use of power for the general welfare. On rationalist and Christian-ethical grounds, he regarded warfare as both senseless and sinful. His thought was in sharp contrast to the ideas of his contemporary, Niccolò Machiavelli, who identified legitimacy with power itself and interpreted peace as a flexible instrument of state.

PEACE THROUGH RATIONAL THOUGHT

As monarchies were established and consolidated in the seventeenth and eighteenth centuries, there emerged a number of proposals for a peace of sovereign equals. These projects were based not only on the ideology of law and on the cultural humanism of the High Renaissance but also on practical considerations. The proposals, assuming that peace could be achieved by the rational organization of international society, variously recommended diplomatic negotiation, mediation, arbitration, an international court, disarmament, and—as a last resort—collective security. Neglecting complex political and economic structures at first, they concentrated on the relationships among rulers.

The general object was to secure international order by a loose confederation of states. This was suggested in 1623 by the French poet and philosopher Emeric Crucé, who called for political and religious tolerance, and recommended a permanent, worldwide organization of ambassadors that would conduct continuous diplomacy. If negotiations failed to settle a conflict, he thought, the member states should enforce a settlement with economic and even military sanctions.

Like Erasmus, Crucé appealed to the noblesse-oblige of princes to implement his plan. In contrast, Maximilien de Béthune, Duc de Sully, proposed to rely on power in order to achieve his "Grand Design" for European peace. Sully attributed his plan to Henry IV of France, under whom he had served until the king's assassination in 1610. Henry had attempted to form a series of European alliances that would reduce the power of the Hapsburgs [royal European family, prominent from the fifteenth to twentieth centuries], but Sully went further, envisioning a European federation. His ideas were familiar to the Quaker philanthropist William Penn. Appealing to economic benefits and to the religious ideal of social harmony, Penn interpreted peace as a practical instrument for social order. He proposed that a confederation of European states should be formed by treaty, rather than by force, and he even recommended that it should include an international tribunal and responsibility for disarmament.

PEACE IS JUST A DREAM?

The concept of confederation was explored early in the eighteenth century by Charles François Irénée Castel de Saint-

Pierre, an abbé and member of the French court, who invented numerous projects for social improvement. In several versions of his "Project for Perpetual Peace," Saint-Pierre elaborated on Sully's "Grand Design," relying on the enlightened self-interest of monarchs to achieve his vision. In mid-century the French philosopher Jean Jacques Rousseau rewrote the abbé's project for publication.

In the process, Rousseau gave the idea of a European confederation its classic expression. As much as he admired Saint-Pierre's proposal, however, Rousseau dismissed it as a noble dream (other philosophers, such as Leibnitz and Voltaire, did not even give it that much dignity). For Rousseau the difficulty was that, like other authors of grand designs, the abbé had neglected the sources of war—economic and cultural interests and the arbitrary power of rulers. The "Project for Perpetual Peace" was itself reasonable, wrote Rousseau, but the contemporary structure of power was not: "One cannot conceive of the possibility of a federative union being established, except by a revolution. And, that granted, who among us would venture to say whether this European federation is to be desired or to be feared."

The idea of enduring peace came to be taken seriously only when it was systematically related to the structure of power. This was accomplished by Immanuel Kant. For this German philosopher peace was an ideal that had the force of history: it was the logical culmination of the extension of civil society from the smallest to the largest units, and it was the condition for self-preservation. Peace was requisite for liberty and social order, and it must embrace all nations. The essential question that Kant addressed, therefore, was not whether there was merit in a federation of nations for peace. He assumed there was. Rather, the interesting problem was the conditions under which federation might be achieved.

Kant framed his essay in the form of a proposed treaty. He identified two approaches. The first one, negative conditions for peace (in the "Preliminary Articles" of the treaty), reflected the familiar just war tradition of limiting the use of violence.

The second approach, positive conditions (in the "Definitive Articles"), was more innovative. It related the mutual interests of nations to open commercial intercourse, and it proposed that they could be constrained from going to war if their governments were constitutional and representative, with a separation of executive and legislative power. Acutely aware of the American and French revolutions, Kant believed that the prospects for peace involved economic and political structures. Enduring peace is possible, he thought, only in a federation of free societies. By relating international peace to changes in the internal distribution of power, Kant anticipated nineteenth-century analyses.

By the time that he wrote his essay, the French Revolution [1777–1799] had yielded another approach: peace through social revolution. Finding the causes of war to be the arbitrary power of monarchs and vested class interests, revolutionaries proclaimed that their movement, however violent, served the cause of peace. As revolutionary France became locked in war with other European powers, it was natural to argue that international order required the liberation of Europe. This idea of peace through revolution would return with force in the twentieth century. . . .

WORLDWIDE PEACE MOVEMENTS

In 1815, as European diplomats gathered in Vienna to liquidate the legacy of the French Revolution and Napoleon, small groups of private citizens in the United States and in England held their own meetings to organize societies opposed to war. Thus began a century of citizen action against war and in favor of a rule of law to solve conflicts among civilized states. By 1914, when World War I broke out, there were peace activists from the Urals to the Rocky Mountains, and in Japan and Australia. What arguments did they develop, and what kinds of societies did they form?

Initially they were religious. Angered at the waste of blood and treasure in twenty-five years of war and revolution in Europe and, to a lesser extent, in the United States, private citizens and religious leaders organized peace societies in New York, Massachusetts, and Ohio in 1815, and in London the next year. Their object was to persuade the public and government leaders that among Christian nations war was not viable, moral, or acceptable. That was the point of the widely distributed essay *A Solemn Review of the Custom of War Showing that War is the Effect of a Popular Delusion and Proposing a Remedy*. In it Noah Worcester, a Unitarian minister and the founder of the Massachusetts Peace Society, blended religious and utilitarian arguments. As the century progressed and peace societies spread from the Atlantic borderlands across the European continent, the early religious rhetoric was muted in favor of secular, practical arguments for a rule of law among civilized nations.

The change from appeals based on the teachings of Jesus Christ to rational, pragmatic, and legalistic arguments is illustrated in a pamphlet by Angelo Umiltà that summarized the work of the Ligue Internationale de la Paix et de la Liberté [International League for Peace and Freedom] (1867–1936). Founded at a stormy congress in Geneva, presided over by the Italian revolutionary and patriot Giuseppe Garibaldi, the league represented the "democratic" or "radical" wing of the continental peace movement. It promoted "civil education" by unofficial citizen groups, and it related international peace to civic and political rights. Efforts were made from 1864 to 1869 to collaborate with the First International [a Socialist association based on the ideas of Karl Marx], but they failed because radical democrats and socialists disagreed on the essentials of democracy.

CHANGES IN THE PATH TO PEACE

Women's involvement in peace activism became ever more common during the nineteenth century. In Germany, whose culture was then hostile to advocates of both feminism and peace, the labors of Margarethe Leonore Selenka led to an explosion of support from women's associations for the Hague Peace Conference of 1899. Selenka coordinated an international women's campaign that collected several million signatures on petitions and held demonstrations in Europe, North America, and Japan. Afterward, she summarized women's strategy to encourage diplomats to take the Hague Conference agenda seriously. Her observation that pacifism was a natural issue for women became a widely shared view among middle-class peace advocates before World War I.

The argument that peace could be achieved through education also became increasingly familiar as public education expanded. In the United States early in the twentieth century, Lucia Ames Mead added peace education to the women's and social issues about which she was active. Believing in the gradual transformation of public opinion, she urged a new curriculum to train teachers and their students in the principles of the rule of law. In particular, she offered a new definition of patriotism and a vision of history that emphasized common human achievements in place of martial and political chronologies. Mead's initiatives were similar to those undertaken by women teachers active in the peace movements of Great Britain, France, Italy, Belgium, and to a lesser extent, Germany.

Imperialist Policies Cause War

WILLIAM JENNINGS BRYAN

William Jennings Bryan was active in American politics from 1890 until his death in 1925. During that time, he served as a U.S. congressman for two terms, held the position of U.S. secretary of state, was a three-time Democratic presidential nominee, and became an active member of the Anti-Imperialist League—America's first citizen organization to openly challenge the government's foreign policy.

Anti-imperialist philosophy held that nations that sought to control colonial empires inevitably ended up embroiled in bloody wars far from their homes—wars that would eventually lead to the collapse of the empire. In this selection, originally published in 1899, Bryan argues that imperialist actions are counterproductive for the success and health of the United States. Bryan highlights the concerns of the anti-imperialists at the end of the eighteenth century about the conclusion of the Spanish-American War in 1898 and the proposed U.S. acquisition of the Philippines. Bryan argues that the extension of American power to foreign lands does not make sense financially, is illegal under American law, and will inevitably lead to war. Finally, he argues that history supports his case.

The anti-imperialists were one of the earliest organized antiwar groups in the United States. They organized groups of citizens to loudly petition the government to end policies that they believed perpetuated violence. The anti-imperialist philosophy has continued to be fundamental to the antiwar movement and is evident in the debates surrounding World War I, Vietnam, and the 2003 war in Iraq.

William Jennings Bryan, "Will It Pay?" *New York Journal*, January 15, 1899.

On former occasions I have quoted authority against the policy of imperialism and have insisted that the adoption of an European colonial policy would endanger the perpetuity of the republic. While every lover of his country should be willing to surrender a pecuniary advantage, however alluring, if that advantage would in the least jeopardize our national existence, still the opponents of imperialism are fortunate in having upon their side the dollar argument as well as the arguments based upon fundamental principles.

The forcible annexation of the Philippine Islands (and, in my judgment, even annexation by the consent of the people) would prove a source of pecuniary loss rather than gain. Heretofore our acquisitions have been confined to the North American continent, the Nation having in view either security from attack or land suitable for settlement. Generally both objects have been realized. Florida and the territory between the Mississippi and the Pacific were necessary for purposes of defense, and, in addition thereto, furnished homes and occupation for an increasing population.

The Hawaiian Islands are nearer to the western than to the eastern hemisphere, and their annexation was urged largely upon the ground that their possession by another nation would be a menace to the United States. When objection was made to the heterogeneous character of the people of the islands, it was met by the assertion that they were few in number. In the opinion of those who favored the annexation of Hawaii the advantages to be gained from a strategical standpoint outweighed the objection raised to the population. No argument made in favor of the annexation of the Hawaiian Islands can be used in support of the imperialistic policy. The purchase of Alaska removed one more monarchy from American territory and gave to the United States a maximum of land with a minimum of inhabitants.

In the forcible annexation of the Philippines our Nation neither adds to its strength nor secures broader opportunities for the American people.

Even if the principle of conquest were permissible under

American public law, the conquest of territory so remote from our shores, inhabited by people who have no sympathy with our history or our customs, and who resent our attempt to overthrow their declaration of independence, would be a tax upon our military and naval strength the magnitude of which cannot now be determined.

Who can estimate in money and men the cost of subduing and keeping in subjection eight millions of people, six thousand miles away, scattered over twelve hundred islands and living under a tropical sun? . . .

If this question is to be settled upon the basis of dollars and cents, who will insure the Nation that the receipts will equal the expenditures? Who will guarantee that the income from the Philippines, be it great or small, will find its way back to the pockets of the people who, through taxation, will furnish the money?

And even if the amount invested in ships, armament and in the equipment of soldiers is returned dollar for dollar, who will place a price upon the blood that will be shed? If war is to be waged for trade, how much trade ought to be demanded in exchange for a human life? And will the man who expects to secure the trade risk his own life or the life of some one else?

The demand for a standing army of one hundred thousand men is the beginning of a policy which will increase the hours of toil and fill the homes of the land with vacant chairs.

COLONIES BRING WAR, TROUBLE, STRIFE

In his essay on the West Indies, [British] Lord Macaulay denies that colonies are a source of profit even to European countries. He says:

> There are some who assert that, in a military and political point of view, the West Indies are of great importance to this country. This is a common but a monstrous misrepresentation. We venture to say that colonial empire has been one of the greatest curses of modern Europe. What nation has it ever strengthened? What nation has it ever enriched? What have been its fruits? Wars of frequent occurrence and

immense cost, fettered trade, lavish expenditure, clashing jurisdiction, corruption in governments and indigence among the people. What have Mexico and Peru done for Spain, the Brazils for Portugal, Batavia for Holland? Or, if the experience of others is lost upon us, shall we not profit by our own? What have we not sacrificed to our infatuated passion for transatlantic dominion? This it is that has so often led us to risk our own smiling gardens and dear firesides for some snowy desert or infectious morass on the other side of the globe; this induced us to resign all the advantages of our insular situation—to embroil ourselves in the intrigues, and fight the battles of half the continent—to form coalitions which were instantly broken—and to give subsidies which were never earned; this gave birth to the fratricidal war against American liberty, with all its disgraceful defeats, and all its barren victories, and all the massacres of the Indian hatchet, and all the bloody contracts of the Hessian slaughterhouse [mercenary soldiers frequently hired for use in wars]; this it was which, in the war against the French republic [the French and Indian War], induced us to send thousands and tens of thousands of our bravest troops to die in West Indian hospitals, while the armies of our enemies were pouring over the Rhine and the Alps. When a colonial acquisition has been in prospect, we have thought no expenditure extravagant, no interference perilous. Gold has been to us as dust, and blood as water. Shall we never learn wisdom? Shall we never cease to prosecute a pursuit wilder than the wildest dream of alchemy, with all the credulity and all the profusion of Sir Epicure Mammon [a fictional character who died selfishly while lying to save his reputation]?

Those who maintain that settlements so remote conduce to the military or maritime power of nations fly in the face of history.

Thus wrote England's orator, statesman and historian.

We Must Learn from History

Shall we refuse to profit by the experience of others? Has the victory of seventy millions of people over seventeen millions so infatuated us with our own prowess that gold is to become to us also as dust and blood as water?

Let us consider for a moment the indirect cost of annexation. Grave domestic problems press for solution; can we afford to neglect them in order to engage unnecessarily in controversies abroad?

Must the people at large busy themselves with the contemplation of "destiny" while the special interests hedge themselves about with legal bulwarks and exact an increasing toll from productive industry?

WARS ABROAD WILL DIVERT ENERGY FROM OUR HOME

While the American people are endeavoring to extend an unsolicited sovereignty over remote peoples, foreign financiers will be able to complete the conquest of our own country. Labor's protest against the black-list and government by injunction, and its plea for arbitration, shorter hours and a fair share of the wealth which it creates, will be drowned in noisy disputes over new boundary lines and in the clash of conflicting authority.

Monopoly can thrive in security so long as the inquiry "Who will haul down the flag," on distant islands turns public attention away from the question, who will uproot the trusts [monopolies] at home?

What will it cost the people to substitute contests over treaties for economic issues? What will it cost the people to postpone consideration of remedial legislation while the ship of state tosses about in the whirlpool of international politics?

In considering the question of imperialism we have a right to weigh possibilities as well as certainties, and among the possibilities may be mentioned an offensive and defensive union between the United States and one or more European nations. Already one may hear an Anglo-American alliance suggested—a suggestion which would have been discarded as a dream a year ago. When this nation abandons its traditions and enters upon a colonial policy, a long step will have been taken toward those entanglements against which Washington and

Jefferson with equal emphasis warned their countrymen.

What a charge the imperialistic idea has already wrought in the minds of its advocates! During the Nation's infancy and development the American people spurned the thought of foreign alliance and its attendant obligations; they refused to yoke the young republic with a monarchy. The wisest among us are not able to measure the cost of a policy which would surrender the Nation's independence of action and drag it into the broils of Europe and Asia.

The Monroe doctrine [President James Monroe's 1823 statement that the United States would not intervene in European affairs and European nations must stay out of American affairs] too, what will become of it? How can we expect European nations to respect our supremacy in the western hemisphere if we insist upon entering Asia? So long as we confine ourselves to our own continent we are strong enough to repel the world; but are we prepared (or is it worth while to prepare) to wage an offensive warfare in other parts of the globe?

On the other hand, what advantages are suggested by imperialists to offset the cost and dangers mentioned?

ARE THERE BENEFITS TO IMPERIALISM?

They tell us that trade follows the flag and that wider markets will be the result of annexation. Without admitting that any argument based upon trade advantages can justify an attempt to adopt a double standard in government—a government by consent in America and a government by force in Asia—it may be answered that commerce is a matter of cost and not a matter of bunting. The protectionist understands this and demands not a flag barrier but a price barrier between the home manufacturer and the foreign competitor.

Public attention has already been called to the fact that, while Spain was sending soldiers to the Philippines, England was sending merchandise. While the home government was sending money to the islands Great Britain was drawing money from them.

The cost of transportation is an important factor and has

more influence than sovereignty in directing the course of trade.

Canada does not refuse to deal with us merely because she flies the British Jack [flag]; in fact, I have been told that she sometimes buys even her British Jacks in the United States. Our foreign trade is increasing, and that increase is not due to an expanding sovereignty.

ARE TRADE ARGUMENTS TRUE?

The insignificance of the trade argument will be manifest to any one who will compare the consuming capacity of the Filipinos with that of a like number of Americans. The inhabitants of the torrid zones can never equal, or even approach, the inhabitants of the temperate zones as customers. England's commerce with the United States is greater than her commerce with India, and yet India has a population of nearly three hundred millions, and the English flag floats over them.

It is yet to be decided whether the open door policy will be adopted in the Orient or a tariff wall built around our subjects there, but neither plan will be found satisfactory. Our people, however, should not expect a colonial policy to prove acceptable, either to the governed or to the governing. If we attempt to run our country upon the European plan we must prepare ourselves for continual complaint. History has thus far failed to furnish a single example of a nation selfish enough to desire a colony and yet unselfish enough to govern it wisely at long range.

It has been argued that annexation would furnish a new field for the investment of American capital. If there is surplus money seeking investment, why is it not employed in the purchase of farm lands, in developing domestic enterprises or in replacing foreign capital? In 1896 we were told that we were dependent upon foreign capital and must so legislate as to keep what we had and invite more. Strange that it should be necessary to have an English financial system in order to bring European capital into the States and also an English colonial policy for the purpose of taking American capital out. Every dollar sent to the Philippines must be withdrawn from present investments, and we must either suffer to the extent of the amount withdrawn or borrow abroad and increase our bondage to foreign money-lenders.

WILL AMERICANS LIVE ABROAD?

It is sometimes suggested that the Philippines would furnish homes for those who are crowded out of this country. This argument, too, is without foundation. The population of the United States amounts to only twenty-one persons to the square mile, while the Philippine Islands already contain about sixty to the square mile. It will be several generations before the population of the United States will be as dense as it is now in the Philippines.

Our people will not flock to Manila; climatic conditions will be as great an obstacle as over-population. English supremacy in India has continued for nearly a hundred and fifty years, and yet in 1891 the British-born population of India was only 100,551—less than the total number of prisoners confined in the jails of India at the end of 1895.

Jamaica has had all the advantages which could be derived from an English colonial policy, and yet the white population in 1891 numbered less than fifteen thousand out of a total of 639,000.

Java has been under the dominion of the Netherlands for nearly three hundred years, and yet in 1894 the Europeans upon the island numbered less than 60,000 out of a total population of more than 25,000,000.

Spain has been able to induce but a small number of her people to settle in the Philippines, and, if we can judge from the reports sent back by our volunteers, we shall not succeed any better.

WHAT ARE THE INTERESTS OF OUR PEOPLE?

But while the Philippines will not prove inviting to Americans, we shall probably draw a considerable number from the islands to the United States. The emigration will be eastward rather than westward. During the six years from 1889 to 1894 more than ninety thousand coolies left India, and we may expect an influx of Malays.

It is not strange that the laboring men should look with undisguised alarm upon the prospect of oriental competition upon the farms and in the factories of the United States. Our people have legislated against Chinese emigration, but to exclude a few Chinese and admit many Filipinos is like straining at a gnat and swallowing a camel.

The farmers and laboring men constitute a large majority of the American people; what is there in annexation for them? Heavier taxes, Asiatic emigration and an opportunity to furnish more sons for the army.

Will it pay?

On Civil Disobedience

HENRY DAVID THOREAU

Although he is most widely known as the author of *Walden*, Henry David Thoreau was also an activist and avid sociopolitical thinker. In 1894, he refused to pay the poll tax to the U.S. federal government as an act of civil disobedience in protest of both the practice of slavery and the Mexican War, which Thoreau felt were unjustifiable.

Thoreau's act of civil disobedience quickly became a public matter, to which he responded with the essay *On Civil Disobedience*, originally delivered as a lecture. In this extract from his essay, Thoreau argues that the state is made up of men (and women) who support it on a daily basis through their actions and economic activity. Thus, the most effective method to change the policies of the government is through civil disobedience, which could include a refusal to pay taxes, perform jobs, or provide economic support.

Thoreau's concept of civil disobedience was enormously influential on Mahatma Gandhi and Martin Luther King Jr. Gandhi, King, and many other leaders of antiwar movements have embraced Thoreau's idea that noncooperation is the best method to confront evil governments, laws, or actions. Examples of Thoreau's influence can be seen in the Montgomery, Alabama, bus boycott in 1955, draft card burnings in the 1960s, refusals to pay taxes that will finance war, and other forms of protest.

I heartily accept the motto, "That government is best which governs least;" and I should like to see it acted up to more rapidly and systematically. Carried out, it finally amounts to this, which also I believe,—"That government is best which governs not at all;" and when men are prepared for it, that will

Henry David Thoreau, lecture, Concord Lyceum, January 26, 1848.

be the kind of government which they will have. Government is at best but an expedient; but most governments are usually, and all governments are sometimes, inexpedient. The objections which have been brought against a standing army, and they are many and weighty, and deserve to prevail, may also at last be brought against a standing government. The standing army is only an arm of the standing government. The government itself, which is only the mode which the people have chosen to execute their will, is equally liable to be abused and perverted before the people can act through it. Witness the present Mexican war, the work of comparatively a few individuals using the standing government as their tool; for, in the outset, the people would not have consented to this measure.

This American government,—what is it but a tradition, though a recent one, endeavoring to transmit itself unimpaired to posterity, but each instant losing some of its integrity? It has not the vitality and force of a single living man; for a single man can bend it to his will. It is a sort of wooden gun to the people themselves. But it is not the less necessary for this; for the people must have some complicated machinery or other, and hear its din, to satisfy that idea of government which they have. Governments show thus how successfully men can be imposed on, even impose on themselves, for their own advantage. It is excellent, we must all allow. Yet this government never of itself furthered any enterprise, but by the alacrity with which it got out of its way. It does not keep the country free. It does not settle the West. It does not educate. The character inherent in the American people has done all that has been accomplished; and it would have done somewhat more, if the government had not sometimes got in its way. For government is an expedient by which men would fain succeed in letting one another alone; and, as has been said, when it is most expedient, the governed are most let alone by it. Trade and commerce, if they were not made of india-rubber, would never manage to bounce over the obstacles which legislators are continually putting in their way; and, if one were to judge these men wholly by the effects of their actions and not partly by their intentions, they would deserve to be classed and punished with those mischievous persons who put obstructions on the railroads.

I ASK FOR A BETTER GOVERNMENT

But, to speak practically and as a citizen, unlike those who call themselves no-government men, I ask for, not at once no government, but *at once* a better government. Let every man make known what kind of government would command his respect, and that will be one step toward obtaining it.

After all, the practical reason why, when the power is once in the hands of the people, a majority are permitted, and for a long period continue, to rule is not because they are most likely to be right, nor because this seems fairest to the minority, but because they are physically the strongest. But a government in which the majority rule in all cases cannot be based on justice, even as far as men understand it. Can there not be a government in which majorities do not virtually decide right and wrong, but conscience?—in which majorities decide only those questions to which the rule of expediency is applicable? Must the citizen ever for a moment, or in the least degree, resign his conscience to the legislator? Why has every man a conscience, then? I think that we should be men first, and subjects afterward. It is not desirable to cultivate a respect for the law, so much as for the right. The only obligation which I have a right to assume is to do at any time what I think right. It is truly enough said that a corporation has no conscience; but a corporation of conscientious men is a corporation *with* a conscience. Law never made men a whit more just; and, by means of their respect for it, even the well-disposed are daily made the agents of injustice. A common and natural result of an undue respect for law is, that you may see a file of soldiers, colonel, captain, corporal, privates, powder-monkeys, and all, marching in admirable order over hill and dale to the wars, against their wills, ay, against their common sense and consciences, which makes it very steep marching indeed, and produces a palpitation of the heart. They have no doubt that it is a damnable business in which they are concerned; they are all peaceably inclined. Now, what are they? Men at all? or small movable forts and magazines, at the service of some unscrupulous man in power? Visit the Navy-Yard, and behold a marine, such a man as an American government can make, or such as it can make a man with its black arts,—a mere shadow and reminiscence of humanity, a man laid out alive and standing, and already, as one may say, buried under arms with funeral accompaniments, though it may be,—

Not a drum was heard, not a funeral note, As his corse to the rampart we hurried; Not a soldier discharged his farewell shot O'er the grave where our hero we buried.

The mass of men serve the state thus, not as men mainly, but as machines, with their bodies. They are the standing army, and the militia, jailers, constables, *posse comitatus*, etc. In most cases there is no free exercise whatever of the judgment or of the moral sense; but they put themselves on a level with wood and earth and stones; and wooden men can perhaps be manufactured that will serve the purpose as well. Such command no more respect than men of straw or a lump of dirt. They have the same sort of worth only as horses and dogs. Yet such as these even are commonly esteemed good citizens. Others—as most legislators, politicians, lawyers, ministers, and office-holders serve the state chiefly with their heads; and, as they rarely make any moral distinctions, they are as likely to serve the devil, without *intending* it, as God. A very few—as heroes, patriots, martyrs, reformers in the great sense, and *men*—serve the state with their conscience also, and so necessarily resist it for the most part; and they are commonly treated as enemies by it. A wise man will only be useful as a man, and will not submit to be "clay," and "stop a hole to keep the wind away," but leave that office to his dust at least:—

I am too high-born to be propertied, To be a secondary at control, Or useful serving-man and instrument To any sovereign state throughout the world.

He who gives himself entirely to his fellow-men appears to them useless and selfish; but he who gives himself partially to them is pronounced a benefactor and philanthropist.

MY GOVERNMENT OR THE SLAVE'S GOVERNMENT?

How does it become a man to behave toward this American government to-day? I answer, that he cannot without disgrace be associated with it. I cannot for an instant recognize that political organization as *my* government which is the *slave's* government also.

All men recognize the right of revolution; that is, the right to refuse allegiance to, and to resist, the government, when its tyranny or its inefficiency are great and unendurable. But almost all say that such is not the case now. But such was the case, they think, in the Revolution of '75 [the American Revolution]. If one were to tell me that this was a bad government because it taxed certain foreign commodities brought to its ports, it is most probable that I should not make an ado about it, for I can do without them. All machines have their friction; and possibly this does enough good to counterbalance the evil. At any rate, it is a great evil to make a stir about it. But when the friction comes to have its machine, and oppression and robbery are organized, I say, let us not have such a machine any longer. In other words, when a sixth of the population of a nation which has undertaken to be the refuge of liberty are slaves, and a whole country is unjustly overrun and conquered by a foreign army, and subjected to military law, I think that it is not too soon for honest men to rebel and revolutionize. What makes this duty the more urgent is the fact that the country so overrun is not our own, but ours is the invading army. . . .

I quarrel not with far-off foes, but with those who, near at home, coöperate with, and do the bidding of, those far away, and without whom the latter would be harmless. We are accustomed to say, that the mass of men are unprepared; but improvement is slow, because the few are not materially wiser or better than the many. It is not so important that many should be as good as you, as that there be some absolute goodness somewhere; for that will leave the whole lump. There are thousands who are *in opinion* opposed to slavery and to the war, who yet in effect do nothing to put an end to them; who, esteeming themselves children of Washington and Franklin, sit down with their hands in their pockets, and say that they know not what to do, and do nothing; who even postpone the question of freedom to the question of free trade, and quietly read the prices-current along with the latest advices from Mexico, after dinner, and, it may be, fall asleep over them both. What is the price-current of an honest man and patriot today? They hesitate, and they regret, and sometimes they petition; but they do nothing in earnest and with effect. They will wait, well disposed, for others to remedy the evil, that they may no longer have it to regret. At most, they give only a cheap vote, and a feeble countenance and Godspeed, to the right, as it goes by them. There are nine hundred and ninety-nine patrons of virtue to one virtuous man. But it is easier to deal with the real possessor of a thing than with the temporary guardian of it. . . .

DUTIES OF PATRIOTISM

It is not a man's duty, as a matter of course, to devote himself to the eradication of any, even the most enormous, wrong; he may still properly have other concerns to engage him; but it is his duty, at least, to wash his hands of it, and, if he gives it no thought longer, not to give it practically his support. If I devote myself to other pursuits and contemplations, I must first see, at least, that I do not pursue them sitting upon another man's shoulders. I must get off him first, that he may pursue his contemplations too. See what gross inconsistency is tolerated. I have heard some of my townsmen say, "I should like to have them order me out to help put down an insurrection of the slaves, or to march to Mexico;—see if I would go;" and yet these very men have each, directly by their allegiance, and so indirectly, at least, by their money, furnished a substitute. The soldier is applauded who refuses to serve in an unjust war by those who do not refuse to sustain the unjust government which makes the war; is applauded by those whose own act and authority he disregards and sets at naught; as if the state were penitent to that degree that it hired one to scourge it while it sinned, but not to that degree that it left off sinning for a moment. Thus, under the name of Order and Civil Government, we are all made at last to pay homage to and support our own meanness. After the first blush of sin comes its indifference; and from immoral it becomes, as it were, *un*moral, and not quite unnecessary to that life which we have made.

Henry David Thoreau

The broadest and most prevalent error requires the most disinterested virtue to sustain it. The slight reproach to which the virtue of patriotism is commonly liable, the noble are most likely to incur. Those who, while they disapprove of the character and measures of a government, yield to it their allegiance and support are undoubtedly its most conscientious supporters, and so frequently the most serious obstacles to reform. Some are petitioning the State to dissolve the Union, to disregard the requisitions of the President. Why do they not dissolve it themselves,—the union between themselves and the State,—and refuse to pay their quota into its treasury? Do not they stand in the same relation to the State that the State does to the Union? And have not the same reasons prevented the State from resisting the Union which have prevented them from resisting the State? . . .

Unjust laws exist: shall we be content to obey them, or shall we endeavor to amend them, and obey them until we have succeeded, or shall we transgress them at once? Men generally, under such a government as this, think that they ought to wait until they have persuaded the majority to alter them. They think that, if they should resist, the remedy would be worse than the evil. But it is the fault of the government itself that the remedy *is* worse than the evil. *It* makes it worse. Why is it not more apt to anticipate and provide for reform? Why does it not cherish its wise minority? Why does it cry and resist before it is hurt? Why does it not encourage its citizens to be on the alert to point out its faults, and *do* better than it would have them? Why does it always crucify Christ, and excommunicate Copernicus and Luther, and pronounce Washington and Franklin rebels?

One would think, that a deliberate and practical denial of its authority was the only offence never contemplated by government; else, why has it not assigned its definite, its suitable and proportionate, penalty? If a man who has no property refuses but once to earn nine shillings for the State, he is put in prison for a period unlimited by any law that I know, and determined only by the discretion of those who placed him there; but if he should steal ninety times nine shillings from the State, he is soon permitted to go at large again.

If the injustice is part of the necessary friction of the machine of government, let it go, let it go: perchance it will wear smooth,—certainly the machine will wear out. If the injustice has a spring, or a pulley, or a rope, or a crank, exclusively for itself, then perhaps you may consider whether the remedy will not be worse than the evil; but if it is of such a nature that it requires you to be the agent of injustice to another, then, I say, break the law. Let your life be a counter-friction to stop the machine. What I have to do is to see, at any rate, that I do not lend myself to the wrong which I condemn.

NEW WAYS FOR CHANGE

As for adopting the ways which the State has provided for remedying the evil, I know not of such ways. They take too much time, and a man's life will be gone. I have other affairs to attend to. I came into this world, not chiefly to make this a good place to live in, but to live in it, be it good or bad. A man has not everything to do, but something; and because he cannot do *everything*, it is not necessary that he should do *something* wrong. It is not my business to be petitioning the Governor or the Legislature any more than it is theirs to petition me; and if they should not hear my petition, what should I do then? But in this case the State has provided no way: its very Constitution is the evil. This may seem to be harsh and stubborn and unconciliatory; but it is to treat with the utmost kindness and consideration the only spirit that can appreciate or deserve it. So is all change for the better, like birth and death, which convulse the body.

I do not hesitate to say, that those who call themselves Abolitionists should at once effectually withdraw their support, both in person and property, from the government of Massachusetts, and not wait till they constitute a majority of one, before they suffer the right to prevail through them. I think that it is enough if they have God on their side, without waiting for that other one. Moreover, any man more right than his neighbors constitutes a majority of one already.

I meet this American government, or its representative, the State government, directly, and face to face, once a year—no more—in the person of its tax-gatherer; this is the only mode in which a man situated as I am necessarily meets it; and it then says distinctly, Recognize me; and the simplest, the most effectual, and, in the present posture of affairs, the indispensablest mode of treating with it on this head, of expressing your little satisfaction with and love for it, is to deny it then. My civil neighbor, the tax-gatherer, is the very man I have to deal with,—for it is, after all, with men and not with parchment that I quarrel,—and he has voluntarily chosen to be an agent of the government. How shall he ever know well what he is and does as an officer of the government, or as a man, until he is obliged to consider whether he shall treat me, his neighbor, for whom he has respect, as a neighbor and well-disposed man, or as a maniac and disturber of the peace, and see if he can get over this obstruction to his neighborliness without a ruder and more impetuous thought or speech corresponding with his action. . . .

CIVIL DISOBEDIENCE

Under a government which imprisons any unjustly, the true place for a just man is also a prison. The proper place to-day, the only place which Massachusetts has provided for her freer and less desponding spirits, is in her prisons, to be put out and locked out of the State by her own act, as they have already put themselves out by their principles. It is there that the fugitive slave, and the Mexican prisoner on parole, and the Indian come to plead the wrongs of his race should find them; on that separate, but more free and honorable, ground, where the State places those who are not *with* her, but *against* her,—the only house in a slave State in which a free man can abide with honor. If any think that their influence would be lost there, and their voices no longer afflict the ear of the State, that they would not be as an enemy within its walls, they do not know by how much truth is stronger than error, nor how much more eloquently and effectively he can combat injustice who has experienced a little in his own person. Cast your whole vote, not a strip of paper merely, but your whole influence. A minority is powerless while it conforms to the majority; it is not even a minority then; but it is irresistible when it clogs by its whole weight. If the alternative is to keep all just men in prison, or give up war and slavery, the State will not hesitate which to choose. If a thousand men were not to pay their tax-bills this year, that would not be a violent and bloody measure, as it would be to pay them, and enable the State to commit violence and shed innocent blood. This is, in fact, the definition of a peaceable revolution, if any such is possible. If the tax-gatherer, or any other public officer, asks me, as one has done, "But what shall I do?" my answer is, "If you really wish to do anything, resign your office." When the subject has refused allegiance, and the officer has resigned his office, then the revolution is accomplished. But even suppose blood should flow. Is there not a sort of bloodshed when the conscience is wounded? Through this wound a man's real manhood and immortality flow out, and he bleeds to an everlasting death. I see this blood flowing now. . . .

Some years ago, the State met me in behalf of the Church, and commanded me to pay a certain sum toward the support of a clergyman whose preaching my father attended, but never I myself. "Pay," it said, "or be locked up in the jail." I declined to pay. But unfortunately, another man saw fit to pay it. I did not see why the schoolmaster should be taxed to support the priest, and not the priest the schoolmaster; for I was not the State's schoolmaster, but I supported myself by voluntary subscription. I did not see why the lyceum should not present its tax-bill, and have the State to back its demand, as well as the Church. However, at the request of the selectmen, I condescended to make some such statement as this in writing:—"Know all men by these presents, that I, Henry Thoreau, do not wish to be regarded as a member of any incorporated society which I have not joined." This I gave to the town clerk; and he has it. The State, having thus learned that I did not wish to be regarded as a member of that church, has never made a like demand on me since; though it said that it must adhere to its original presumption that time. If I had known how to name them, I should then have signed off in detail from all the societies which I never signed on to; but I did not know where to find a complete list.

I have paid no poll-tax for six years. I was put into a jail once on this account, for one night; and, as I stood considering the walls of solid stone, two or three feet thick, the door of wood and iron, a foot thick, and the iron grating which strained the light, I could not help being struck with the foolishness of that institution which treated me as if I were mere flesh and blood and bones, to be locked up. I wondered that it should have concluded at length that this was the best use it could put me to, and had never thought to avail itself of my services in some way. I saw that, if there was a wall of stone between me and my townsmen, there was a still more difficult one to climb or break through before they could get to be as free as I was. I did not for a moment feel confined, and the walls seemed a great waste of stone and mortar. I felt as if I alone of all my townsmen had paid my tax. They plainly did not know how to treat me, but behaved like persons who are underbred. In every threat and in every compliment there was a blunder; for they thought that my chief desire was to stand the other side of that stone wall. I could not but smile to see how industriously they locked the door on my meditations, which followed them out again without let or hindrance, and *they* were really all that was dangerous. As they could not reach me, they had resolved to punish my body; just as boys, if they cannot come at some person against whom they have a spite, will abuse his dog. I saw that the State was half-witted, that it was timid as a lone woman with her silver spoons, and that it did not know its friends from its foes, and I lost all my remaining respect for it, and pitied it. . . .

I have never declined paying the highway tax, because I am as desirous of being a good neighbor as I am of being a bad subject; and as for supporting schools, I am doing my part to educate my fellow-countrymen now. It is for no particular item in the tax-bill that I refuse to pay it. I simply wish to refuse allegiance to the State, to withdraw and stand aloof from it effectually. I do not care to trace the course of my dollar, if I could, till it buys a man or a musket to shoot one with,—the dollar is innocent,—but I am concerned to trace the effects of my allegiance. In fact, I quietly declare war with the State, after my fashion, though I will still make what use and get what advantage of her I can, as is usual in such cases.

The authority of government, even such as I am willing to submit to,—for I will cheerfully obey those who know and can do better than I, and in many things even those who neither know nor can do so well,—is still an impure one: to be strictly just, it must have the sanction and consent of the governed. It can have no pure right over my person and property but what I concede to it. The progress from an absolute to a limited monarchy, from a limited monarchy to a democracy, is a progress toward a true respect for the individual. Even the Chinese philosopher was wise enough to regard the individual as the basis of the empire. Is a democracy, such as we know it, the last improvement possible in government? Is it not possible to take a step further towards recognizing and organizing the rights of man? There will never be a really free and enlightened State until the State comes to recognize the individual as a higher and independent power, from which all its own power and authority are derived, and treats him accordingly. I please myself with imagining a State at last which can afford to be just to all men, and to treat the individual with respect as a neighbor; which even would not think it inconsistent with its own repose if a few were to live aloof from it, not meddling with it, nor embraced by it, who fulfilled all the duties of neighbors and fellow-men. A State which bore this kind of fruit, and suffered it to drop off as fast as it ripened, would prepare the way for a still more perfect and glorious State, which also I have imagined, but not yet anywhere seen.

CHAPTER 2

FROM WORLD WAR I TO THE NUCLEAR AGE

AMERICAN
SOCIAL
MOVEMENTS

Americans Protest World War I

HOWARD ZINN

As the United States entered World War I, a large percentage of Americans were unsupportive of what appeared to be a war to control colonies and establish international influence. During World War I, such antiwar views were considered dangerous to American interests, and despite the existence of the First Amendment, the U.S. government attempted to silence political challengers who spoke out against the war. This was accomplished through laws that served to limit dissent and place limits on the First Amendment's strength. In this selection, historian Howard Zinn details the history of America's entry into World War I and the antiwar movement against it.

As professor of history and political science first at Spelman College in Atlanta and currently at Boston University, Howard Zinn is best known for his book *A People's History of the United States.* In it, he tells America's history from the perspective of the masses—the working poor, women, African Americans, Native Americans, and immigrant laborers. This perspective has become central to the antiwar movement, which has adopted Zinn's position that official histories have often focused only on the achievements of the upper crust of society—presidents, business leaders, and military leaders— at the expense of those who bore the brunt of the burdens of war.

"War is the health of the state," the radical writer Randolph Bourne said, in the midst of the First World War. Indeed, as the nations of Europe went to war in 1914, the governments flourished, patriotism bloomed, class struggle was stilled, and young men died in frightful numbers on the battlefields—often for a hundred yards of land, a line of trenches. . . .

Howard Zinn, *A People's History of the United States: 1492–Present.* New York: Harper-Collins, 1999. Copyright © 1980 by Howard Zinn. All rights reserved. Reproduced by permission of the publisher.

Ten million [soldiers] were to die on the battlefield; 20 million [people] were to die of hunger and disease related to the war. And no one since that day has been able to show that the war brought any gain for humanity that would be worth one human life. The rhetoric of the socialists, that it was an "imperialist war," now seems moderate and hardly arguable. The advanced capitalist countries of Europe were fighting over boundaries, colonies, spheres of influence; they were competing for Alsace-Lorraine, the Balkans, Africa, the Middle East.

The war came shortly after the opening of the twentieth century, in the midst of exultation (perhaps only among the elite in the Western world) about progress and modernization. One day after the English declared war, [English author] Henry James wrote to a friend: "The plunge of civilization into this abyss of blood and darkness . . . is a thing that so gives away the whole long age during which we have supposed the world to be . . . gradually bettering." In the first Battle of the Marne, the British and French succeeded in blocking the German advance on Paris. Each side had 500,000 casualties.

THE WAR AND THE NEWS

The killing started very fast, and on a large scale. In August 1914, a volunteer for the British army had to be 5 feet 8 inches to enlist. By October, the requirement was lowered to 5 feet 5 inches. That month there were thirty thousand casualties, and then one could be 5 feet 3. In the first three months of war, almost the entire original British army was wiped out. . . .

Back home, the British were not told of the slaughter. One English writer recalled: "The most bloody defeat in the history of Britain . . . might occur . . . and our Press come out bland and copious and graphic with nothing to show that we had not had quite a good day—a victory really. . . ." The same thing was happening on the German side; as Erich Maria Remarque wrote in his great novel, on days when men by the thousands were being blown apart by machine guns and shells, the official dispatches announced "All Quiet on the Western Front."

In July 1916, British General Douglas Haig ordered eleven

divisions of English soldiers to climb out of their trenches and move toward the German lines. The six German divisions opened up with their machine guns. Of the 110,000 who attacked, 20,000 were killed, 40,000 more wounded—all those bodies strewn on no man's land, the ghostly territory between the contending trenches. On January 1, 1917, Haig was promoted to field marshal. . . .

The people of France and Britain were not told the extent of the casualties. When, in the last year of the war, the Germans attacked ferociously on the Somme, and left 300,000 British soldiers dead or wounded, London newspapers printed the following, we learn from Paul Fussell's *The Great War and Modern Memory:*

WHAT CAN I DO?
How the Civilian May Help in this Crisis.
Be cheerful. . . .
Write encouragingly to friends at the front. . . .
Don't repeat foolish gossip.
Don't listen to idle rumors.
Don't think you know better than Haig.

Into this pit of death and deception came the United States, in the spring of 1917. Mutinies were beginning to occur in the French army. Soon, out of 112 divisions, 68 would have mutinies; 629 men would be tried and condemned, 50 shot by firing squads. American troops were badly needed.

THE UNITED STATES ENTERS THE WAR

President Woodrow Wilson had promised that the United States would stay neutral in the war: "There is such a thing as a nation being too proud to fight." But in April of 1917, the Germans had announced they would have their submarines sink any ship bringing supplies to their enemies; and they had sunk a number of merchant vessels. Wilson now said he must stand by the right of Americans to travel on merchant ships in the war zone. "I cannot consent to any abridgement of the rights of American citizens in any respect. . . ."

It was unrealistic to expect that the Germans should treat the United States as neutral in the war when the U.S. had been shipping great amounts of war materials to Germany's enemies. In early 1915, the British liner *Lusitania* was torpedoed and sunk by a German submarine. She sank in eighteen minutes, and 1,198 people died, including 124 Americans. The United States claimed the *Lusitania* carried an innocent cargo, and therefore the torpedoing was a monstrous German atrocity. Actually, the *Lusitania* was heavily armed: it carried 1,248 cases of 3-inch shells, 4,927 boxes of cartridges (1,000 rounds in each box), and 2,000 more cases of small-arms ammunition. Her manifests were falsified to hide this fact, and the British and American governments lied about the cargo. . . .

In 1914 a serious recession had begun in the United States. [Financier] J.P. Morgan later testified: "The war opened during a period of hard times. . . . Business throughout the country was depressed, farm prices were deflated, unemployment was serious, the heavy industries were working far below capacity and bank clearings were off." But by 1915, war orders for the Allies (mostly England) had stimulated the economy, and by April 1917 more than $2 billion worth of goods had been sold to the Allies. As Hofstadter says: "America became bound up with the Allies in a fateful union of war and prosperity."

Prosperity depended much on foreign markets, it was believed by the leaders of the country. In 1897, the private foreign investments of the United States amounted to $700 million dollars. By 1914 they were $3½ billion. Wilson's Secretary of State, William Jennings Bryan, while a believer in neutrality in the war, also believed that the United States needed overseas markets; in May of 1914 he praised the President as one who had "opened the doors of all the weaker countries to an invasion of American capital and American enterprise."

A WAR FOR MORE MONEY?

Back in 1907, Woodrow Wilson had said in a lecture at Columbia University: "Concessions obtained by financiers must be safeguarded by ministers of state, even if the sovereignty of unwilling nations be outraged in the process. . . . the doors of the nations which are closed must be battered down." In his 1912 campaign he said: "Our domestic markets no longer suffice, we need foreign markets." In a memo to Bryan he described his aim as "an open door to the world," and in 1914 he said he supported "the righteous conquest of foreign markets."

With World War I, England became more and more a market for American goods and for loans at interest. J. P. Morgan and Company acted as agents for the Allies, and when, in 1915, Wilson lifted the ban on private bank loans to the Allies, Morgan could now begin lending money in such great amounts as to both make great profit and tie American finance closely to the interest of a British victory in the war against Germany.

The industrialists and the political leaders talked of prosperity as if it were classless, as if everyone gained from Morgan's loans. True, the war meant more production, more employment, but did the workers in the steel plants gain as much as U.S. Steel, which made $348 million in profit in 1916 alone? When the United States entered the war, it was the rich who took even more direct charge of the economy. Financier Bernard Baruch headed the War Industries Board, the most powerful of the wartime government agencies. Bankers, railroad men, and industrialists dominated these agencies. . . .

American capitalism needed international rivalry—and periodic war—to create an artificial community of interest between rich and poor, supplanting the genuine community of interest among the poor that showed itself in sporadic movements. How conscious of this were individual entrepreneurs and statesmen? That is hard to know. But their actions, even if half-conscious, instinctive drives to survive, matched such a scheme. And in 1917 this demanded a national consensus for war.

THE U.S. GOVERNMENT'S WAR AT HOME

The government quickly succeeded in creating such a consensus, according to the traditional histories. Woodrow Wilson's biographer Arthur Link wrote: "In the final analysis

American policy was determined by the President and public opinion." In fact, there is no way of measuring public opinion at that time, and there is no persuasive evidence that the public wanted war. The government had to work hard to create its consensus. That there was no spontaneous urge to fight is suggested by the strong measures taken: a draft of young men, an elaborate propaganda campaign throughout the country, and harsh punishment for those who refused to get in line.

Despite the rousing words of Wilson about a war "to end all wars" and "to make the world safe for democracy," Americans did not rush to enlist. A million men were needed, but in the first six weeks after the declaration of war only 73,000 volunteered. Congress voted overwhelmingly for a draft.

George Creel, a veteran newspaperman, became the government's official propagandist for the war; he set up a Committee on Public Information to persuade Americans the war was right. It sponsored 75,000 speakers, who gave 750,000 four-minute speeches in five thousand American cities and towns. It was a massive effort to excite a reluctant public. At the beginning of 1917, a member of the National Civic Federation had complained that "neither workingmen nor farmers" were taking "any part or interest in the efforts of the security or defense leagues or other movements for national preparedness."

AMERICAN CHALLENGES

The day after Congress declared war, the Socialist party met in emergency convention in St. Louis and called the declaration "a crime against the people of the United States." In the summer of 1917, Socialist antiwar meetings in Minnesota drew large crowds—five thousand, ten thousand, twenty thousand farmers—protesting the war, the draft, profiteering. A local newspaper in Wisconsin, the Plymouth *Review*, said that probably no party ever gained more rapidly in strength than the Socialist party just at the present time." It reported that "thousands assemble to hear Socialist speakers in places where ordinarily a few hundred are considered large assemblages."

The Akron *Beacon-Journal,* a conservative newspaper in Ohio, said there was "scarcely a political observer . . . but what will admit that were an election to come now a mighty tide of socialism would inundate the Middle West." It said the country had "never embarked upon a more unpopular war."

In the municipal elections of 1917, against the tide of propaganda and patriotism, the Socialists made remarkable gains. Their candidate for mayor of New York, Morris Hillquit, got 22 percent of the vote, five times the normal Socialist vote there. Ten Socialists were elected to the New York State legislature. In Chicago, the party vote went from 3.6 percent in 1915 to 34.7 percent in 1917. In Buffalo, it went from 2.6 percent to 30.2 percent. . . .

Congress passed, and Wilson signed, in June of 1917, the Espionage Act. From its title one would suppose it was an act against spying. However, it had a clause that provided penalties up to twenty years in prison for "Whoever, when the United States is at war, shall wilfully cause or attempt to cause insubordination, disloyalty, mutiny, or refusal of duty in the military or naval forces of the United States, or shall wilfully obstruct the recruiting or enlistment service of the U.S. . . ." Unless one had a theory about the nature of governments, it was not clear how the Espionage Act would be used. It even had a clause that said "nothing in this section shall be construed to limit or restrict . . . any discussion, comment, or criticism of the acts or policies of the Government. . . ." But its double-talk concealed a singleness of purpose. The Espionage Act was used to imprison Americans who spoke or wrote against the war.

THE FIRST AMENDMENT?

Two months after the law passed, a Socialist named Charles Schenck was arrested in Philadelphia for printing and distributing fifteen thousand leaflets that denounced the draft law and the war. The leaflet recited the Thirteenth Amendment provision against "involuntary servitude" and said the Conscription Act violated this. Conscription, it said, was "a monstrous deed against humanity in the interests of the financiers of Wall Street." And: "Do not submit to intimidation."

Schenck was indicted, tried, found guilty, and sentenced to six months in jail for violating the Espionage Act. (It turned out to be one of the shortest sentences given in such cases.) Schenck appealed, arguing that the Act, by prosecuting speech and writing, violated the First Amendment: "Congress shall make no law . . . abridging the freedom of speech, or of the press. . . ."

The Supreme Court's decision was unanimous and was written by its most famous liberal, Oliver Wendell Holmes. He summarized the contents of the leaflet and said it was undoubtedly intended to "obstruct" the carrying out of the draft law. Was Schenck protected by the First Amendment? Holmes said:

> The most stringent protection of free speech would not protect a man in falsely shouting fire in a theatre and causing a panic. . . . The question in every case is whether the words used are used in such circumstances and are of such a nature as to create a clear and present danger that they will bring about the substantive evils that Congress has a right to prevent.

Holmes's analogy was clever and attractive. Few people would think free speech should be conferred on someone shouting fire in a theater and causing a panic. But did that example fit criticism of the war? Zechariah Chafee, a Harvard law school professor, wrote later (Free Speech in the United States) that a more apt analogy for Schenck was someone getting up between the acts at a theater and declaring that there were not enough fire exits. To play further with the example: was not Schenck's act more like someone shouting, not falsely, but truly, to people about to buy tickets and enter a theater, that there was a fire raging inside?

Perhaps free speech could not be tolerated by any reasonable person if it constituted a "clear and present danger" to life and liberty; after all, free speech must compete with other vital rights. But was not the war itself a "clear and present danger," indeed, more clear and more present and more dangerous to life than any argument against it? Did citizens not have a right to object to war, a right to be a danger to dangerous policies? . . .

A WAR ON FREE SPEECH

The case of Eugene Debs soon came before the Supreme Court. In June of 1918, Debs visited three Socialists who were in prison for opposing the draft, and then spoke, across the street from the jail, to an audience he kept enthralled for two hours. He was one of the country's great orators, and was interrupted again and again by laughter and applause. . . .

> They tell us that we live in a great free republic; that our institutions are democratic; that we are a free and self-governing people. That is too much, even for a joke. . . .
>
> Wars throughout history have been waged for conquest and plunder. . . . And that is war in a nutshell. The master class has always declared the wars; the subject class has always fought the battles. . . .

Debs was arrested for violating the Espionage Act. There were draft-age youths in his audience, and his words would "obstruct the recruiting or enlistment service.". . .

Debs refused at his trial to take the stand in his defense, or to call a witness on his behalf. He denied nothing about what he said. But before the jury began its deliberations, he spoke to them:

> I have been accused of obstructing the war. I admit it. Gentlemen, I abhor war. I would oppose war if I stood alone. . . . I have sympathy with the suffering, struggling people everywhere. It does not make any difference under what flag they were born, or where they live. . . .

The jury found him guilty of violating the Espionage Act. Debs addressed the judge before sentencing:

> Your honor, years ago I recognized my kinship with all living beings, and I made up my mind that I was not one bit better than the meanest on earth. I said then, and I say now,

that while there is a lower class, I am in it; while there is a criminal element, I am of it; while there is a soul in prison, I am not free.

The judge denounced those "who would strike the sword from the hand of this nation while she is engaged in defending herself against a foreign and brutal power." He sentenced Debs to ten years in prison. . . .

About nine hundred people went to prison under the Espionage Act. This substantial opposition was put out of sight, while the visible national mood was represented by military bands, flag waving, the mass buying of war bonds, the majority's acquiescence to the draft and the war. This acquiescence was achieved by shrewd public relations and by intimidation—an effort organized with all the power of the federal government and the money of big business behind it. The magnitude of that campaign to discourage opposition says something about the spontaneous feelings of the population toward the war.

THE ROLE OF THE MEDIA

The newspapers helped create an atmosphere of fear for possible opponents of the war. In April of 1917, the *New York Times* quoted Elihu Root (former Secretary of War, a corporation lawyer) as saying: "We must have no criticism now." A few months later it quoted him again that "there are men walking about the streets of this city tonight who ought to be taken out at sunrise tomorrow and shot for treason." At the same time, Theodore Roosevelt was talking to the Harvard Club about Socialists, IWWs [International Workers of the World], and others who wanted peace as "a whole raft of sexless creatures."...

The national press cooperated with the government. The *New York Times* in the summer of 1917 carried an editorial: "It is the duty of every good citizen to communicate to proper authorities any evidence of sedition that comes to his notice." And the *Literary Digest* asked its readers "to clip and send to us any editorial utterances they encounter which seem to them seditious or treasonable." Creel's Committee on Public Information advertised that people should "report the man who spreads pessimistic stories. Report him to the Department of Justice." In 1918, the Attorney General said: "It is safe to say that never in its history has this country been so thoroughly policed."

Why these huge efforts? On August 1, 1917, the New York *Herald* reported that in New York City ninety of the first hundred draftees claimed exemption. In Minnesota, headlines in the Minneapolis *Journal* of August 6 and 7 read: "Draft Opposition Fast Spreading In State," and "Conscripts Give False Addresses." In Florida, two Negro farm hands went into the woods with a shotgun and mutilated themselves to avoid the draft: one blew off four fingers of his hand; the other shot off his arm below the elbow. Senator Thomas Hardwick of Georgia said "there was undoudtedly general and widespread opposition on the part of many thousands . . . to the enactment of the draft law. Numerous and largely attended mass meetings held in every part of the State protested against it. . . ." Ultimately, over 330,000 men were classified as draft evaders. . . .

On July 1, 1917, radicals organized a parade in Boston against the war, with banners:

IS THIS A POPULAR WAR, WHY CONSCRIPTION?
WHO STOLE PANAMA? WHO CRUSHED HAITI?
WE DEMAND PEACE.

The New York *Call* said eight thousand people marched, including "4000 members of the Central Labor Union, 2000 members of the Lettish Socialist Organizations, 1500 Lithuanians, Jewish members of cloak trades, and other branches of the party." The parade was attacked by soldiers and sailors, on orders from their officers.

A COORDINATED ATTACK ON FREE SPEECH

The Post Office Department began taking away the mailing privileges of newspapers and magazines that printed antiwar articles. *The Masses*, a socialist magazine of politics, literature, and art, was banned from the mails. It had carried an editorial by Max Eastman in the summer of 1917, saying, among other things: "For what specific purposes are you shipping our bodies, and the bodies of our sons, to Europe? For my part, I do not recognize the right of a government to draft me to a war whose purposes I do not believe in."

In Los Angeles, a film was shown that dealt with the American Revolution and depicted British atrocities against the colonists. It was called *The Spirit of '76*. The man who made the film was prosecuted under the Espionage Act because, the judge said, the film tended "to question the good faith of our ally, Great Britain." He was sentenced to ten years prison. The case was officially listed as *U.S. v. Spirit of '76*. . . .

Schools and universities discouraged opposition to the war. At Columbia University, J. McKeen Cattell, a psychologist, a long-time critic of the Board of Trustees' control of the university, and an opponent of the war, was fired. A week later, in protest, the famous historian Charles Beard resigned from the Columbia faculty, charging the trustees with being "reactionary and visionless in politics, narrow and medieval in religion. . . ."

In Congress, a few voices spoke out against the war. The first woman in the House of Representatives, Jeannette Rankin, did not respond when her name was called in the roll call on the declaration of war. One of the veteran politicians of the House, a supporter of the war, went to her and whispered, "Little woman, you cannot afford not to vote. You represent the womanhood of the country. . . ." On the next roll call she stood up: "I want to stand by my country, but I cannot vote for war. I vote No." A popular song of the time was: "I Didn't Raise My Boy to Be a Soldier." It was overwhelmed, however, by songs like "Over There," "It's a Grand Old Flag," and "Johnny Get Your Gun."

Socialist Kate Richards O'Hare, speaking in North Dakota in July of 1917, said, it was reported, that "the women of the United States were nothing more nor less than brood sows, to raise children to get into the army and be made into fertilizer."

She was arrested, tried, found guilty, and sentenced to five years in the Missouri state penitentiary. . . .

THE GREAT WAR ENDS

The war ended in November 1918. Fifty thousand American soldiers had died, and it did not take long, even in the case of patriots, for bitterness and disillusionment to spread through the country. This was reflected in the literature of the postwar decade. . . .

Ernest Hemingway would write *A Farewell to Arms*. Years later a college student named Irwin Shaw would write a play, *Bury the Dead*. And a Hollywood screenwriter named Dalton Trumbo would write a powerful and chilling antiwar novel about a torso and brain left alive on the battlefield of World War I, *Johnny Got His Gun*. Ford Madox Ford wrote *No More Parades*.

With all the wartime jailings, the intimidation, the drive for national unity, when the war was over, the Establishment still feared socialism. . . .

THE INTERNAL CLEANUP

In January 1920, four thousand persons were rounded up all over the country, held in seclusion for long periods of time, brought into secret hearings, and ordered deported. In Boston, Department of Justice agents, aided by local police, arrested six hundred people by raiding meeting halls or by invading their homes in the early morning. A troubled federal judge described the process:

> Pains were taken to give spectacular publicity to the raid, and to make it appear that there was great and imminent public danger. . . . The arrested aliens, in most instances perfectly quiet and harmless working people, many of them not long ago Russian peasants, were handcuffed in pairs, and then, for the purposes of transfer on trains and through the streets of Boston, chained together. . . .

In the spring of 1920, a typesetter and anarchist named Andrea Salsedo was arrested in New York by FBI agents and held for eight weeks in the FBI offices on the fourteenth floor of the Park Row Building, not allowed to contact family or friends or lawyers. Then his crushed body was found on the pavement below the building and the FBI said he had committed suicide by jumping from the fourteenth floor window. Two friends of Salsedo, anarchists and workingmen in the Boston area, having just learned of his death, began carrying guns. They were arrested on a streetcar in Brockton, Massachusetts, and charged with a holdup and murder that had taken place two weeks before at a shoe factory. These were Nicola Sacco and Bartolomeo Vanzetti. They went on trial, were found guilty, and spent seven years in jail while appeals went on, and while all over the country and the world, people became involved in their case. The trial record and the surrounding circumstances suggested that Sacco and Vanzetti were sentenced to death because they were anarchists and foreigners. In August 1927, as police broke up marches and picket lines with arrests and beatings, and troops surrounded the prison, they were electrocuted.

Sacco's last message to his son Dante, in his painfully learned English, was a message to millions of others in the years to come:

So, Son, instead of crying, be strong, so as to be able to comfort your mother . . . take her for a long walk in the quiet country, gathering wild flowers here and there. . . . But remember always, Dante, in the play of happiness, don't you use all for yourself only. . . . help the persecuted and the victim because they are your better friends. . . . In this struggle of life you will find more and love and you will be loved.

There had been reforms. The patriotic fervor of war had been invoked. The courts and jails had been used to reinforce the idea that certain ideas, certain kinds of resistance, could not be tolerated. And still, even from the cells of the condemned, the message was going out: the class war was still on in that supposedly classless society, the United States.

The Minorities of the World Want Peace and Freedom

W.E.B. Du Bois

As World War II ended, the United States entered the Cold War with the USSR, and fear of communism ran high. American leaders were focused on military solutions to prevent the spread of communism from the Soviet bloc. Within this context, antiwar activists were viewed as potentially threatening to American interests and were suspected of possible Communist sympathies.

Undaunted by a climate that stressed conformity over dissent, African American leader W.E.B. Du Bois spoke out against war and racism in America. In this transcript of his keynote address at the 1949 Waldorf-Astoria Peace Conference, Du Bois speaks about his commitment to nonviolent resistance to war and outlines what he sees as the future for all minorities across the world.

Du Bois was the first African American to receive a Ph.D. from Harvard. By 1949 he had more than fifty years of experience as an author, professor, editor, and activist. An admirer of the Soviet Union, Du Bois advocated the spread of socialism and joined the American Communist Party in 1961. Disenchanted with the United States, he emigrated to Ghana, where he died in 1963.

This Cultural and Scientific Conference for World Peace has been a success. In a time of hysteria, suspicion and hate, we have succeeded in bringing face to face in friendly meetings, one of the largest gatherings of creative artists and thinkers the world has seen; and it would have been quite the largest if all who wished to come were here. Meeting together

W.E.B. Du Bois, "Peace: Freedom's Road for Oppressed Peoples," *Worker*, April 17, 1949, pp. 7–10.

for three full days, we have found wide agreement and sympathy, we have established ideals and friendships belting the globe. We have not and are not now in complete agreement on all matters. But in one vital respect our agreement is complete: No More War! The horrible world-old habit of wholesale murder of those who disagree with us is, we are convinced, a relic of barbarism bound to destroy our best culture unless it is absolutely and definitely abolished.

On the other hand, we are not childishly deceived as to the enormity of the task of organizing and conducting a peaceful world. We are many minds and backgrounds, separated not only by space but by the terrible barriers of language and social patterns; we face deliberate crime, ignorance and misunderstanding . . . but we firmly believe that the greatest of these is misunderstanding. Decent wage, health and schools will one day reduce crime and ignorance to manageable proportions. It is in the vast realm of misunderstanding, misrepresentation and doubt, that war is born and flourishes.

Perhaps unwittingly, the opposition which our effort has incurred proves this truth with startling clarity. We know and the saner nation knows that we are not traitors nor conspirators; and far from plotting force and violence it is precisely force and violence that we bitterly oppose. This conference was not called to defend Communism nor Socialism nor the American way of life. It was called to promote peace! It was called to say and say again that no matter how right or wrong differing systems of belief in religion, industry or government may be, war is not the method by which their differences can successfully be settled for the good of mankind.

To the defense of this absolutely indisputable thesis, proven by oceans of blood and worlds of human suffering, we have invited the cooperation of all men; and that cooperation to abolish war does not compel or even ask men to surrender their opinions. It simply insists that force is not reason and beliefs cannot be changed by suppression. . . .

But there is one aspect of our conference which has forced itself upon the attention of us all. That is the effort of the press and certain leaders of public opinion to spread the idea that some persons here are by their beliefs and actions so beyond the pale of humanity as to deserve neither sympathy nor confidence. Particularly have the people of the Soviet Union been singled out for something bordering on insult and repeatedly accused of warmongering and aggression.

I do not pretend to be an expert on Russia, but seeing what the press can do to a conference like this in misinterpretation and distortion, I wonder if what is called aggression in the Balkans may not be liberation of landless serfs and giving their ignorant masses in 25 years such education as American Negro slaves have not received in 75; and of sending their former masters not to the legislature but scurrying over the earth like rats distributing lies.

W.E.B. Du Bois

All this I do not know but it can be true. And I do know that, if the press has lied about Russia as it has lied about American Negroes for three hundred years, I for one will condemn neither Russia nor Communism on such testimony.

THE PLIGHT OF THE MAJORITY

But beyond and above this there arises before this conference the plight and cause of the vast majority of mankind who are not white. These colored races, the Chinese, Japanese, Indians and Indonesians; the peoples of Africa, many of those of South America and most of those of the Caribbean, with fifteen million Negroes of the United States—these are the vast majority of mankind whose condition and future are the crucial test of the attitudes of those peoples who today demand mastery of the world. Secluded for the most part in colonies or dominated areas, they have been enslaved and insulted, kicked in the teeth and used for the rape and exploitation of the British, French, Dutch, Belgium, Spanish and Italian empires.

This great America, this vast and rich land around you is built on the slavery, toil and degradation of Africans. Here until well into the second half of the nineteenth century they were sold like cattle. And New York did not stop to picket abolitionists; they tarred, feathered and killed them. Today in this land we have risen from the dead not to full manhood and citizenship, but to the place where we can at least stand and yell our own protest. We thank the America that helped us.

But we know well that unless we had helped ourselves we would still in New York City be exactly where our brothers are in Mississippi, where I ride in Jim Crow cars and would be kicked out of any hotel or public library. When such a nation arraigns Russia, all that I with the best will can remember is that the Soviet Union alone of all modern nations has prohibition of race and color discrimination written into its fundamental law, and that unlike similar words in our Constitution their law is enforced. . . .

THE STAKE OF DARKER PEOPLES IN PEACE

I saw the birth of the League of Nations and I sat in San Francisco when the United Nations was born. In both instances I worked and pled for the darker peoples, particularly those in imperialist colonies. We got mandates at Geneva which meant nothing. We got trusteeships at San Francisco and there again a determined blocking of all real meaning of colonial freedom by the united effort of Great Britain and the United States, and the sole opposition of Russia. Again in the Marshall Plan [the U.S effort to aid Western Europe after World War II] the nations helped are the colonial imperialists and no colored people unless, like [Chinese Nationalist leader] Chiang Kai-shek, they are puppets of world exploiting investors.

I tell you people of America, the dark world is on the move! It wants and will have freedom, autonomy and equality. It will not be diverted in these fundamental rights by dialectical splitting of political hairs. We know what the Atlantic Pact [NATO] proposes for the protection of colonial serfs of European imperialists. We know why Italy has been promised Ethiopia's territory by the [U.S.] Department of State. We know why the President of the United States goes fishing when the charter of Negro American rights is laughed to death by Democrats and Republicans, and lynching and disfranchisement go merrily on. We know all this and so does every dark man on earth. The white race may, if it will, tax itself into poverty, and arm itself for suicide, but the vast majority of mankind will march on and over them to freedom and self-rule.

But this catastrophe is the last which we of the darker world wish or will. We have no time for revenge or for sneering at white men's tragic mistakes. What we want is a decent world, where a man does not have to have a white skin in order to be a man. Where poverty is not a means to wealth, where ignorance is not used to prove race superiority, where sickness and death are not part of our factory system.

And all this depends first on world peace.

Peace is not an end. It is the gateway to real civilization. With peace all things may be added. With war, we destroy even that which the toil and sacrifice of ages have builded.

The Antinuclear, Antiwar Manifesto

BERTRAND RUSSELL AND ALBERT EINSTEIN

Ten years after the 1945 U.S. atomic bombing of Hiroshima and Nagaski in Japan, Bertrand Russell and Albert Einstein cowrote what would become the cornerstone of the antinuclear movement. The Russell-Einstein Manifesto, excerpted below, is a call for scientists and governments to unite and work toward peaceful conflict resolution while denouncing the use of nuclear weapons. The language and goals of the Russell-Einstein Manifesto soon became the central ideology of the antinuclear movement, which defined the antiwar movement throughout the 1950s.

Russell and Einstein were both noted for their pacifist views. In addition, both were former Nobel Prize laureates—Einstein in physics in 1921 and Russell in literature in 1950. Einstein first wrote to President Harry Truman in 1939 to warn him of the power of atomic energy and to warn of the destructive possibilities if Nazi Germany were to develop atomic weapons before the United States. Although he had not been involved in the development of these weapons, Einstein realized that scientists did not fully understand the effects of nuclear weapons and feared that the world was rushing toward certain self-destruction.

As a professor of philosophy at Cambridge University in England, Bertrand Russell was noted for both his progressive views on society and his groundbreaking work in the field of logic. When he denounced both sides during World War I, he was fired and imprisoned. Russell soon became an outspoken critic of war. Upon learning of the development of nuclear weapons, he promptly began organizing both within England and internationally to end their production.

I n the tragic situation which confronts humanity, we feel that scientists should assemble in conference to appraise the perils that have arisen as a result of the development of weapons of mass destruction, and to discuss a resolution in the spirit of the appended draft.

We are speaking on this occasion, not as members of this or that nation, continent, or creed, but as human beings, members of the species Man, whose continued existence is in doubt. The world is full of conflicts; and, overshadowing all minor conflicts, the titanic struggle between Communism and anti-Communism.

Almost everybody who is politically conscious has strong feelings about one or more of these issues; but we want you, if you can, to set aside such feelings and consider yourselves only as members of a biological species which has had a remarkable history, and whose disappearance none of us can desire.

We shall try to say no single word which should appeal to one group rather than to another. All, equally, are in peril, and, if the peril is understood, there is hope that they may collectively avert it.

WE MUST PREVENT WAR

We have to learn to think in a new way. We have to learn to ask ourselves, not what steps can be taken to give military victory to whatever group we prefer, for there no longer are such steps; the question we have to ask ourselves is: what steps can be taken to prevent a military contest of which the issue must be disastrous to all parties?

The general public, and even many men in positions of authority, have not realized what would be involved in a war with nuclear bombs. The general public still thinks in terms of the obliteration of cities. It is understood that the new bombs are more powerful than the old, and that, while one A-bomb could obliterate Hiroshima, one H-bomb could obliterate the largest cities, such as London, New York, and Moscow.

No doubt in an H-bomb war great cities would be obliterated. But this is one of the minor disasters that would have to be faced. If everybody in London, New York, and Moscow were exterminated, the world might, in the course of a few centuries, recover from the blow. But we now know, especially since the Bikini test [U.S. Navy tests in which nuclear weapons were exploded. The Bikini Islands had to be evacuated and parts of the area still contain radioactive contamination.] that nuclear bombs can gradually spread destruction over a very much wider area than had been supposed.

It is stated on very good authority that a bomb can now be manufactured which will be 2,500 times as powerful as that which destroyed Hiroshima. Such a bomb, if exploded near the ground or under water, sends radio-active particles into the upper air. They sink gradually and reach the surface of the earth in the form of a deadly dust or rain. It was this dust which infected the Japanese fishermen and their catch of fish.

AN END TO THE HUMAN RACE?

No one knows how widely such lethal radio-active particles might be diffused, but the best authorities are unanimous in saying that a war with H-bombs might possibly put an end to the human race. It is feared that if many H-bombs are used there will be universal death, sudden only for a minority, but for the majority a slow torture of disease and disintegration.

Many warnings have been uttered by eminent men of science and by authorities in military strategy. None of them will say that the worst results are certain. What they do say is that these results are possible, and no one can be sure that they will not be realized. We have not yet found that the views of experts on this question depend in any degree upon their politics or prejudices. They depend only, so far as our researches have revealed, upon the extent of the particular expert's knowledge. We have found that the men who know most are the most gloomy.

Here, then, is the problem which we present to you, stark and dreadful and inescapable: Shall we put an end to the human race; or shall mankind renounce war? People will not face this alternative because it is so difficult to abolish war.

The abolition of war will demand distasteful limitations of national sovereignty. But what perhaps impedes understanding of the situation more than anything else is that the term "mankind" feels vague and abstract. People scarcely realize in imagination that the danger is to themselves and their children and their grandchildren, and not only to a dimly apprehended humanity. They can scarcely bring themselves to grasp that they, individually, and those whom they love are in imminent danger of perishing agonizingly. And so they hope that perhaps war may be allowed to continue provided modern weapons are prohibited.

This hope is illusory. Whatever agreements not to use H-bombs had been reached in time of peace, they would no longer be considered binding in time of war, and both sides would set to work to manufacture H-bombs as soon as war broke out, for, if one side manufactured the bombs and the other did not, the side that manufactured them would inevitably be victorious.

Although an agreement to renounce nuclear weapons as part of a general reduction of armaments would not afford an ultimate solution, it would serve certain important purposes. First: any agreement between East and West is to the good in so far as it tends to diminish tension. Second: the abolition of thermo-nuclear weapons, if each side believed that the other had carried it out sincerely, would lessen the fear of a sudden attack in the style of Pearl Harbour, which at present keeps both sides in a state of nervous apprehension. We should, therefore, welcome such an agreement though only as a first step.

Most of us are not neutral in feeling, but, as human beings, we have to remember that, if the issues between East and West are to be decided in any manner that can give any possible satisfaction to anybody, whether Communist or anti-Communist, whether Asian or European or American, whether White or Black, then these issues must not be decided by war. We should wish this to be understood, both in the East and in the West.

Remember Your Humanity

There lies before us, if we choose, continual progress in happiness, knowledge, and wisdom. Shall we, instead, choose death, because we cannot forget our quarrels? We appeal, as human beings, to human beings: Remember your humanity, and forget the rest. If you can do so, the way lies open to a new Paradise; if you cannot, there lies before you the risk of universal death.

Resolution
We invite this Congress, and through it the scientists of
the world and the general public, to subscribe to
the following resolution:

"In view of the fact that in any future world war nuclear weapons will certainly be employed, and that such weapons threaten the continued existence of mankind, we urge the Governments of the world to realize, and to acknowledge publicly, that their purpose cannot be furthered by a world war, and we urge them, consequently, to find peaceful means for the settlement of all matters of dispute between them."

CHAPTER 3

THE 1960s AND THE VIETNAM WAR

AMERICAN
SOCIAL
MOVEMENTS

We Must Work for Peace in Vietnam and America

MARTIN LUTHER KING JR.

As president of the Southern Christian Leadership Conference from 1957 until his assassination in 1968, Martin Luther King Jr. was one of America's leading civil rights activists. Although he was awarded the Nobel Peace Prize in 1964, King was hesitant to speak out against the Vietnam War, fearing that this would divert energy away from the struggle for civil rights. By 1967, King realized that the expense of the Vietnam War was strangling social programs and that minority men were fighting and dying in disproportionate numbers to whites for liberties they did not have at home.

In the following address, delivered on April 4, 1967, at the Riverside Church in New York, King denounces U.S. involvement in the Vietnam War, which he considered an unjust cause. He urges people to protest the government's "disgraceful commitment" to the war and undertake a revolution against poverty, racism, and militarism. He says Americans should work together for a peaceful, just society. In speaking out, King legitimized the antiwar movement for many minorities. Shortly after this speech, large numbers of minorities became involved in the antiwar movement.

I come to this magnificent house of worship tonight because my conscience leaves me no other choice. I join you in this meeting because I am in deepest agreement with the aims and work of the organization which has brought us together, Clergy and Laymen Concerned About Vietnam. The recent statements of your executive committee are the sentiments of

Martin Luther King Jr., address at Riverside Church, New York, April 4, 1967. Copyright © 1967 by the Heirs to the Estate of Martin Luther King Jr. Reproduced by permission of Writers House Inc.

my own heart, and I found myself in full accord when I read its opening lines: "A time comes when silence is betrayal." That time has come for us in relation to Vietnam. . . .

Some of us who have already begun to break the silence of the night have found that the calling to speak is often a vocation of agony, but we must speak. We must speak with all the humility that is appropriate to our limited vision, but we must speak. And we must rejoice as well, for surely this is the first time in our nation's history that a significant number of its religious leaders have chosen to move beyond the prophesying of smooth patriotism to the high grounds of a firm dissent based upon the mandates of conscience and the reading of history. Perhaps a new spirit is rising among us. If it is, let us trace its movement, and pray that our own inner being may be sensitive to its guidance. For we are deeply in need of a new way beyond the darkness that seems so close around us.

Over the past two years, as I have moved to break the betrayal of my own silences and to speak from the burnings of my own heart, as I have called for radical departures from the destruction of Vietnam, many persons have questioned me about the wisdom of my path. At the heart of their concerns, this query has often loomed large and loud: "Why are you speaking about the war, Dr. King? Why are you joining the voices of dissent?" "Peace and civil rights don't mix," they say. "Aren't you hurting the cause of your people?" they ask. And when I hear them, though I often understand the source of their concern, I am nevertheless greatly saddened, for such questions mean that the inquirers have not really known me, my commitment, or my calling. Indeed, their questions suggest that they do not know the world in which they live. In the light of such tragic misunderstanding, I deem it of signal importance to try to state clearly, and I trust concisely, why I believe that the path from Dexter Avenue Baptist Church— the church in Montgomery, Alabama, where I began my pastorate—leads clearly to this sanctuary tonight.

I come to this platform tonight to make a passionate plea to my beloved nation. This speech is not addressed to Hanoi [capital of North Vietnam] or to the National Liberation Front [Vietnamese organization fighting against Americans in Vietnam]. It is not addressed to China or to Russia. Nor is it an attempt to overlook the ambiguity of the total situation and the need for a collective solution to the tragedy of Vietnam. Neither is it an attempt to make North Vietnam or the National Liberation Front paragons of virtue, nor to overlook the role they must play in the successful resolution of the problem. While they both may have justifiable reasons to be suspicious of the good faith of the United States, life and history give eloquent testimony to the fact that conflicts are never resolved without trustful give and take on both sides. Tonight, however, I wish not to speak with Hanoi and the National Liberation Front, but rather to my fellow Americans.

ONE MOVEMENT FOR PEACE

Since I am a preacher by calling, I suppose it is not surprising that I have seven major reasons for bringing Vietnam into the field of my moral vision. There is at the outset a very obvious and almost facile connection between the war in Vietnam and the struggle I and others have been waging in America. A few years ago there was a shining moment in that struggle. It seemed as if there was a real promise of hope for the poor, both black and white, through the poverty program. There were experiments, hopes, new beginnings. Then came the buildup in Vietnam, and I watched this program broken and eviscerated as if it were some idle political plaything of a society gone mad on war. And I knew that America would never invest the necessary funds or energies in rehabilitation of its poor so long as adventures like Vietnam continued to draw men and skills and money like some demonic, destructive suction tube. So I was increasingly compelled to see the war as an enemy of the poor and to attack it as such.

Perhaps a more tragic recognition of reality took place when it became clear to me that the war was doing far more than devastating the hopes of the poor at home. It was sending their sons and their brothers and their husbands to fight and to die in extraordinarily high proportions relative to the rest of the population. We were taking the black young men who had been crippled by our society and sending them eight thousand miles away to guarantee liberties in Southeast Asia which they had not found in southwest Georgia and East Harlem. So we have been repeatedly faced with the cruel irony of watching Negro and white boys on TV screens as they kill and die together for a nation that has been unable to seat them together in the same schools. So we watch them in brutal solidarity burning the huts of a poor village, but we realize that they would hardly live on the same block in Chicago. I could not be silent in the face of such cruel manipulation of the poor.

My third reason moves to an even deeper level of awareness, for it grows out of my experience in the ghettos of the North over the last three years, especially the last three summers. As I have walked among the desperate, rejected, and angry young men, I have told them that Molotov cocktails and rifles would not solve their problems. I have tried to offer them my deepest compassion while maintaining my conviction that social change comes most meaningfully through nonviolent action. But they asked, and rightly so, "What about Vietnam?" They asked if our own nation wasn't using massive doses of violence to solve its problems, to bring about the changes it wanted. Their questions hit home, and I knew that I could never again raise my voice against the violence of the oppressed in the ghettos without having first spoken clearly to the greatest purveyor of violence in the world today: my own government. For the sake of those boys, for the sake of this government, for the sake of the hundreds of thousands trembling under our violence, I cannot be silent.

For those who ask the question, "Aren't you a civil rights leader?" and thereby mean to exclude me from the movement for peace, I have this further answer. In 1957, when a group of us formed the Southern Christian Leadership Conference, we chose as our motto: "To save the soul of America.". . .

Now it should be incandescently clear that no one who has any concern for the integrity and life of America today can ignore the present war. If America's soul becomes totally poisoned, part of the autopsy must read "Vietnam." It can never be saved so long as it destroys the deepest hopes of men the world over. So it is that those of us who are yet determined that "America will be" are led down the path of protest and dissent, working for the health of our land.

As if the weight of such a commitment to the life and health of America were not enough, another burden of responsibility was placed upon me in 1954 [King says "1954" but most likely means 1964, the year he received the Nobel Peace Prize]. And I cannot forget that the Nobel Peace Prize was also a commission, a commission to work harder than I had ever worked before for the brotherhood of man. This is a calling that takes me beyond national allegiances.

But even if it were not present, I would yet have to live with the meaning of my commitment to the ministry of Jesus Christ. To me, the relationship of this ministry to the making of peace is so obvious that I sometimes marvel at those who ask me why I am speaking against the war. Could it be that they do not know that the Good News was meant for all men—for communist and capitalist, for their children and ours, for black and for white, for revolutionary and conservative? Have they forgotten that my ministry is in obedience to the one who loved his enemies so fully that he died for them? What then can I say to the Vietcong [North Vietnam's army] or to Castro [Cuban Communist leader] or to Mao [Chinese Communist leader] as a faithful minister of this one? Can I threaten them with death or must I not share with them my life?

Finally, as I try to explain for you and for myself the road that leads from Montgomery to this place, I would have offered all that was most valid if I simply said that I must be true to my conviction that I share with all men the calling to be a son of the living God. Beyond the calling of race or nation or creed is this vocation of sonship and brotherhood. Because I believe that the Father is deeply concerned, especially for His suffering and helpless and outcast children, I come tonight to speak for them. This I believe to be the privilege and the burden of all of us who deem ourselves bound by allegiances and loyalties which are broader and deeper than nationalism and which go beyond our nation's self-defined goals and positions. We are called to speak for the weak, for the voiceless, for the victims of our nation, for those it calls "enemy," for no document from human hands can make these humans any less our brothers. . . .

THE VIETNAMESE PERSPECTIVE

And as I ponder the madness of Vietnam and search within myself for ways to understand and respond in compassion, my mind goes constantly to the people of that peninsula. I speak now not of the soldiers of each side, not of the ideologies of the Liberation Front, not of the junta in Saigon, but simply of the people who have been living under the curse of war for almost three continuous decades now. I think of them, too, because it is clear to me that there will be no meaningful solution there until some attempt is made to know them and hear their broken cries.

They must see Americans as strange liberators. The Vietnamese people proclaimed their own independence in 1954 in 1945 rather after a combined French and Japanese occupation and before the communist revolution in China. They were led by Ho Chi Minh. Even though they quoted the American Declaration of Independence in their own document of freedom, we refused to recognize them. Instead, we decided to support France in its reconquest of her former colony. Our government felt then that the Vietnamese people were not ready for independence. . . .

For nine years following 1945 we denied the people of Vietnam the right of independence. For nine years we vigorously supported the French in their abortive effort to recolonize Vietnam. Before the end of the war we were meeting eighty percent of the French war costs. Even before the French were defeated at Dien Bien Phu, they began to despair of their reckless action, but we did not. We encouraged them with our huge financial and military supplies to continue the war even after they had lost the will. Soon we would be paying almost the full costs of this tragic attempt at recolonization.

After the French were defeated, it looked as if independence and land reform would come again through the Geneva Agreement [1954 agreement which ended the French war in Vietnam. The Geneva agreement divided Vietnam into two countries]. But instead there came the United States, determined that Ho should not unify the temporarily divided nation, and the peasants watched again as we supported one of the most vicious modern dictators, our chosen man, Premier Diem [leader of South Vietnam widely believed to be subservient to American interests]. The peasants watched and cringed as Diem ruthlessly rooted out all opposition, supported their extortionist landlords, and refused even to discuss reunification with the North. The peasants watched as all of this was presided over by United States influence and then by increasing numbers of United States troops who came to help quell the insurgency that Diem's methods had aroused. When Diem was overthrown they may have been happy, but the long line of military dictators seemed to offer no real change, especially in terms of their need for land and peace.

The only change came from America as we increased our troop commitments in support of governments which were singularly corrupt, inept, and without popular support. All the while the people read our leaflets and received the regular promises of peace and democracy and land reform. Now they languish under our bombs and consider us, not their fellow Vietnamese, the real enemy. . . .

Now there is little left to build on, save bitterness. Soon the only solid physical foundations remaining will be found at our military bases and in the concrete of the concentration camps we call "fortified hamlets." The peasants may well wonder if we plan to build our new Vietnam on such grounds as these. Could we blame them for such thoughts? We must speak for them and raise the questions they cannot raise. These, too, are our brothers.

Perhaps a more difficult but no less necessary task is to speak for those who have been designated as our enemies. What of the National Liberation Front, that strangely anonymous group we call "VC" or "communists"? What must they think of the United States of America when they realize that we permitted the repression and cruelty of Diem, which helped to bring them into being as a resistance group in the South? What do they think of our condoning the violence which led to their own taking up of arms? How can they believe in our integrity when now we speak of "aggression from the North" as if there were nothing more essential to the war? How can they trust us when now we charge them with violence after the murderous reign of Diem and charge them with violence while we pour every new weapon of death into their land? Surely we must understand their feelings, even if we do not condone their actions. Surely we must see that the men we supported pressed them to their violence. Surely we must see that our own computerized plans of destruction simply dwarf their greatest acts.

How do they judge us when our officials know that their membership is less than twenty-five percent communist, and yet insist on giving them the blanket name? What must they be thinking when they know that we are aware of their control of major sections of Vietnam, and yet we appear ready to allow national elections in which this highly organized political parallel government will not have a part? They ask how we can speak of free elections when the Saigon press is censored and controlled by the military junta. And they are surely right to wonder what kind of new government we plan to help form without them, the only party in real touch with the peasants. They question our political goals and they deny the reality of a peace settlement from which they will be excluded. Their questions are frighteningly relevant. Is our nation planning to build on political myth again, and then shore it up upon the power of a new violence?

THE POWER OF UNDERSTANDING

Here is the true meaning and value of compassion and non-violence, when it helps us to see the enemy's point of view, to hear his questions, to know his assessment of ourselves. For from his view we may indeed see the basic weaknesses of our own condition, and if we are mature, we may learn and grow and profit from the wisdom of the brothers who are called the opposition. . . .

Also, it must be clear that the leaders of Hanoi considered the presence of American troops in support of the Diem regime to have been the initial military breach of the Geneva Agreement concerning foreign troops. They remind us that they did not begin to send troops in large numbers and even supplies into the South until American forces had moved into the tens of thousands.

Hanoi remembers how our leaders refused to tell us the truth about the earlier North Vietnamese overtures for peace, how the president claimed that none existed when they had clearly been made. Ho Chi Minh has watched as America has spoken of peace and built up its forces, and now he has surely heard the increasing international rumors of American plans for an invasion of the North. He knows the bombing and shelling and mining we are doing are part of traditional pre-invasion strategy. Perhaps only his sense of humor and of irony can save him when he hears the most powerful nation of the world speaking of aggression as it drops thousands of bombs on a poor, weak nation more than eight hundred, or rather, eight thousand miles away from its shores.

At this point I should make it clear that while I have tried in these last few minutes to give a voice to the voiceless in Vietnam and to understand the arguments of those who are called "enemy," I am as deeply concerned about our own troops there as anything else. For it occurs to me that what we are submitting them to in Vietnam is not simply the brutalizing process that goes on in any war where armies face each other and seek to destroy. We are adding cynicism to the process of death, for they must know after a short period there that none of the things we claim to be fighting for are really involved. Before long they must know that their government has sent them into a struggle among Vietnamese, and the more sophisticated surely realize that we are on the side of the wealthy, and the secure, while we create a hell for the poor.

WE MUST ADDRESS AMERICAN VALUES

Somehow this madness must cease. We must stop now. I speak as a child of God and brother to the suffering poor of Vietnam. I speak for those whose land is being laid waste, whose homes are being destroyed, whose culture is being subverted. I speak for the poor of America who are paying the double price of smashed hopes at home, and dealt death and corruption in Vietnam. I speak as a citizen of the world, for the world as it stands aghast at the path we have taken. I speak as one who loves America, to the leaders of our own nation: The great initiative in this war is ours; the initiative to stop it must be ours. . . .

Now there is something seductively tempting about stopping there and sending us all off on what in some circles has become a popular crusade against the war in Vietnam. I say we must enter that struggle, but I wish to go on now to say something even more disturbing.

The war in Vietnam is but a symptom of a far deeper malady within the American spirit, and if we ignore this sobering reality . . . we will find ourselves organizing "clergy and laymen concerned" committees for the next generation. They will be concerned about Guatemala and Peru. They will be concerned about Thailand and Cambodia. They will be concerned about Mozambique and South Africa. We will be marching for these and a dozen other names and attending rallies without end unless there is a significant and profound change in American life and policy. So such thoughts take us beyond Vietnam, but not beyond our calling as sons of the living God. . . .

It is with such activity in mind that the words of the late John F. Kennedy come back to haunt us. Five years ago he said, "Those who make peaceful revolution impossible will make violent revolution inevitable." Increasingly, by choice or by accident, this is the role our nation has taken, the role of those who make peaceful revolution impossible by refusing to give up the privileges and the pleasures that come from the immense profits of overseas investments. I am convinced that if we are to get on the right side of the world revolution, we as a nation must undergo a radical revolution of values. We must rapidly begin . . . the shift from a thing-oriented society to a person-oriented society. When machines and computers, profit motives and property rights, are considered more important than people, the giant triplets of racism, extreme materialism, and militarism are incapable of being conquered. . . .

A TRUE, POSITIVE REVOLUTION

A true revolution of values will soon look uneasily on the glaring contrast of poverty and wealth. With righteous indignation, it will look across the seas and see individual capitalists of the West investing huge sums of money in Asia, Africa, and South America, only to take the profits out with no concern for the social betterment of the countries, and say, "This is not just." It will look at our alliance with the landed gentry of South America and say, "This is not just." The Western arrogance of feeling that it has everything to teach others and nothing to learn from them is not just.

A true revolution of values will lay hand on the world order and say of war, "This way of settling differences is not just." This business of burning human beings with napalm, of filling our nation's homes with orphans and widows, of injecting poisonous drugs of hate into the veins of peoples normally humane, of sending men home from dark and bloody battlefields physically handicapped and psychologically deranged, cannot be reconciled with wisdom, justice, and love. A nation that continues year after year to spend more money on military defense than on programs of social uplift is approaching spiritual death. . . .

This kind of positive revolution of values is our best defense against communism. War is not the answer. Communism will never be defeated by the use of atomic bombs or nuclear weapons. Let us not join those who shout war and, through their misguided passions, urge the United States to relinquish its participation in the United Nations. These are days which demand wise restraint and calm reasonableness. We must not engage in a negative anticommunism, but rather in a positive thrust for democracy, realizing that our greatest defense against communism is to take offensive action in behalf of justice. We must with positive action seek to remove those conditions of poverty, insecurity, and injustice, which are the fertile soil in which the seed of communism grows and develops.

These are revolutionary times. All over the globe men are revolting against old systems of exploitation and oppression, and out of the wounds of a frail world, new systems of justice and equality are being born. The shirtless and barefoot people of the land are rising up as never before. The people who sat in darkness have seen a great light. We in the West must support these revolutions. . . .

A genuine revolution of values means in the final analysis that our loyalties must become ecumenical rather than sectional. Every nation must now develop an overriding loyalty to mankind as a whole in order to preserve the best in their individual societies. . . .

We are now faced with the fact, my friends, that tomorrow is today. We are confronted with the fierce urgency of now. In this unfolding conundrum of life and history, there is such a thing as being too late. Procrastination is still the thief of time. Life often leaves us standing bare, naked, and dejected with a lost opportunity. The tide in the affairs of men does not remain at flood—it ebbs. We may cry out desperately for time to pause in her passage, but time is adamant to every plea and rushes on. Over the bleached bones and jumbled residues of numerous civilizations are written the pathetic words, "Too late." There is an invisible book of life that faithfully records our vigilance or our neglect. Omar Khayyam is right: "The moving finger writes, and having writ moves on."

We still have a choice today: nonviolent coexistence or violent coannihilation. We must move past indecision to action. We must find new ways to speak for peace in Vietnam and justice throughout the developing world, a world that borders on our doors. If we do not act, we shall surely be dragged down the long, dark, and shameful corridors of time reserved for those who possess power without compassion, might without morality, and strength without sight.

Now let us begin. Now let us rededicate ourselves to the long and bitter, but beautiful, struggle for a new world. This is the calling of the sons of God, and our brothers wait eagerly for our response. Shall we say the odds are too great? Shall we tell them the struggle is too hard? Will our message be that the forces of American life militate against their arrival as full men, and we send our deepest regrets? Or will there be another message—of longing, of hope, of solidarity with their yearnings, of commitment to their cause, whatever the cost? The choice is ours, and though we might prefer it otherwise, we must choose in this crucial moment of human history. . . .

And if we will only make the right choice, we will be able to transform this pending cosmic elegy into a creative psalm of peace. If we will make the right choice, we will be able to transform the jangling discords of our world into a beautiful symphony of brotherhood. If we will but make the right choice, we will be able to speed up the day, all over America and all over the world, when justice will roll down like waters, and righteousness like a mighty stream.

The FBI's Attempts to Stop the Antiwar Movement

JAMES KIRKPATRICK DAVIS

During the 1960s, Presidents Lyndon B. Johnson and Richard Nixon worked with FBI director J. Edgar Hoover to infiltrate and eliminate organized forms of dissent inside America. In this selection James Kirkpatrick Davis guides readers through a tangled web of top-secret documents and leaked information to detail how the FBI developed its infamous Counter Intelligence Program, which it used to illegally spy on and take action against U.S. citizens. COINTELPRO, as it was known, was eventually uncovered, and the FBI was forced to abandon this tactic in 1971.

Davis reveals through White House and FBI correspondences why the U.S. government took such drastic action: The nation's leaders feared that the Communists they were fighting in Vietnam had themselves infiltrated U.S. schools, universities, and social and political organizations. This fear led them to label almost every antiwar group as pro-Communist and to then work to neutralize the group, often through illegal methods.

Davis has authored three books on the FBI. His examination of previously top-secret FBI documents has helped to reveal that targets of COINTELPRO operations included not only groups such as the Communist Party USA and the Ku Klux Klan, but also Martin Luther King Jr., the Students for a Democratic Society, and the "New Left"—a broad term describing a variety of student, African American, and feminist groups.

James Kirkpatrick Davis, *Assault on the Left: The FBI and the Sixties Antiwar Movement.* Westport, CT: Praeger, 1997. Copyright © 1997 by James Kirkpatrick Davis. All rights reserved. Reproduced by permission of Greenwood Publishing Group, Inc.

"They are half-way citizens who are neither morally, mentally or emotionally mature."

—Director John Edgar Hoover

In the summer of 1962, the fledgling Students for a Democratic Society (SDS), the student arm of the League for Industrial Democracy, released to the nation what became [according to writer and activist Kirkpatrick Sale] "the most widely distributed document on the American left in the sixties." The 66-page text, officially known as the *Port Huron Statement of the Students for a Democratic Society*, was drafted during an intensive five-day meeting held at the FDR Camp in Michigan, on the southern shore of Lake Huron.

Eight colleges and universities were represented among the fifty-nine individuals in attendance. There were a number of non-SDS members, groups including the Student Peace Union, the Campus Americans for a Democratic Action, the National Student Christian Foundation, and the Student Nonviolent Coordinating Committee. Those in attendance tended to be idealistic, bright, and well-read, with varying activist experience. Most were from white, privileged backgrounds. . . .

In preparing the Port Huron Statement, the SDS writers, primarily Robert "Al" Haber and Tom Hayden, were attempting to develop an entirely new ideology for what was to become the New Left movement. The New Left, a term coined by C. Wright Mills in 1961, was applied to an advocation of an *evolution* in American politics rather than the revolution advocated by the Old Left for so long with so little success.

The Old Left was considered by the New Left to be out of date and out of step with the new student-based political radicalism of the sixties. The working class, the traditional vanguard for change within the Old Left political philosophy, was seen as simply not up to the task of fostering radical changes in the sixties. The New Left was in large measure a generational rebellion, a rebellion of the young.

The Port Huron Statement was a call to political action. "As a social system we seek the establishment of a democracy of individual participation; governed by two central aims; that the individual share in those social divisions which determine the quality and direction of his life; that society be organized to encourage independence in men and provide the media for their common participation.". . .

Individual Americans, according to the statement, were living lives that were alienated from the very government they were paying taxes to support. Individual citizens, living in the world's richest country in the world's oldest republic, were unable to control their own lives. The power to make social, economic, and political decisions must be made by citizens directly affected by those decisions. There must be a true participatory democracy. The nation's enormously overgrown power apparatus should be the object of reform at every level. The document advocated a total evolution in the nation's social, economic, and political machinery to more directly benefit individual citizens.

On global matters, the Port Huron Statement opposed the unyielding anti-communism of the United States while also castigating the aggressiveness of the Warsaw Pact nations. It urged rapprochement among the major powers and expanded assistance to the Third World.

The New Left concept of action was by no means new in 1962. Protest activities occurred across America well before the Port Huron Conference. Demonstrations with varying degrees of coordination and effectiveness had been directed against racial segregation in the South, against the arms race, against atomic testing, against the growing American military industrial complex, against war, and against the intrusiveness of the House Committee on Un-American Activities.

But Port Huron was epochal in the history of American radical politics. It marked, as scholar Howard Taylor has said, "a turning point in American political history, the point at which a coalition of student movements had become possible and a radical student movement had been formed." The SDS would, before the decade was over, include pacifist, religious, civil rights, and disarmament groups as well as elements of the Old Left. . . .

American Forces in Vietnam

During that same summer of 1962, American forces in South Vietnam numbered twelve hundred. John F. Kennedy was then in the second year of his presidency and he was the third American president to be concerned about the future of Vietnam. It had been seventeen years since the first American was killed there and three years since the killing of the first American on military assignment.

By 1962, J. Edgar Hoover had been director of the Federal Bureau of Investigation for thirty-eight years. Although the official authorization for domestic counterintelligence operations against the New Left would not be issued for another six years, it seems certain that he was informed of the Port Huron meeting from the beginning.

In the early sixties, the New Left was most conspicuously represented by a few active SDS chapters on college campuses. These early chapters, having almost no influence on a national scale, were loosely associated with a dozen or more similar types of domestic-based political action groups. By the end of the decade, however, the New Left would be associated with literally hundreds of protest organizations with hundreds of thousands of active participants. The anti-Vietnam War crusade, spearheaded by the New Left influence, came to represent a political and sociological phenomenon almost certainly unmatched in the history of American politics. . . .

The Protests Begin

The first small protests against American involvement in Vietnam appeared in 1963. The Student Peace Union carried signs against the war during the Easter Peace Walk in New York City. In August 1963, American pacifists displayed signs condemning America's Vietnam involvement during the annual ceremony commemorating the Hiroshima-Nagasaki atomic bombing of 1945. That summer in Philadelphia, members of the Student Peace Union carried signs in front of the city's downtown federal building. In September, the executive board of the Committee for a Sane Nuclear Policy issued a national press release urging "disengagement" in Vietnam. In October, the Friends Committee on National Legislation (the Congressional Quaker Lobby) opened the Vietnam Information Center in Washington, D.C. The first campus demonstrations occurred at several colleges during the fall 1963 speaking tour of Mme. Dinh Nhu, the sister-in-law of Ngo Dinh Diem, the president of South Vietnam.

By the end of 1963 there were over 15,000 American military advisors serving in Vietnam. American aid to Vietnam in 1963 exceeded $500 million. By March of 1964, U.S. troops had been increased to more than 20,000, and over 500 U.S. servicemen had been killed while acting as advisors to the South Vietnamese Army.

In April of 1964, over two hundred members of the Women's International League for Peace and Freedom met in Washington to discuss Vietnam. The organization issued a press release which called for an immediate withdrawal of American forces and a convening of the Geneva Conference at the earliest possible date. Soon after, the *National Guardian* carried a large advertisement signed by almost one hundred college students saying flatly that they would refuse military service in Vietnam. In late May a similar advertisement was carried by the *New York Herald Tribune*.

The maneuverings of the Johnson administration in Vietnam were approved by seven out of ten Americans. Most antiwar dissidents, still very small in number, thought that a much larger American involvement was simply a matter of time. They viewed the conflict as a civil war that could not be "won" by the United States by any rational definition of the word....

THE FBI BECOMES MORE AGGRESSIVE

In February of 1962, the nation's capitol was the site of a joint demonstration against the testing of atomic weapons, organized by the Student Peace Union and the Students for a Turn Toward Peace. Later that spring, pacifists attempted to interfere with U.S. atomic testing in the Christmas Islands.

In April of 1962, the FBI began its campaign of arranging

for Internal Revenue Service (IRS) investigations of left-wing organizations and individual organization members. These targets were selected for investigation because of their political activity and not because they had necessarily violated tax laws. . . .

On May 2, 1964, a group of about one thousand students, most of whom had attended a war protest conference in March at Yale University, held two demonstrations in New York. The larger contingent marched to the United Nations Plaza to hear speeches denouncing the U.S. involvement in Vietnam. Police broke up both demonstrations and arrested about fifty students. This group, known as the May 2 Committee, included members of the Progressive Labor Movement [PLM], who were extreme in their opposition to the war. The FBI had been monitoring the committee. In late April, special agents and customs officials raided the headquarters of the PLM and seized a "Vietcong [North Vietnam's army] propaganda film."

Activist Dave Dellinger organized an antiwar demonstration on July 3, 1964, in Lafayette Park, across the street from the White House. Those taking part included, among others, Joan Baez, Reverend Phillip Berrigan, Reverend Daniel Berrigan, A.J. Muste, and Rabbi Abraham Feinberg. At the conclusion of the demonstration the group walked across the street. Dave Dellinger remembers, "We walked to the fence and kneeled down in front of the White House. It was supposed to be an act of civil disobedience but they didn't arrest us."

Several days later, on July 10, 1964, a petition signed by more than five thousand college instructors was hand delivered at the State Department. It called for the United States to make every effort to secure a neutralized North and South Vietnam "protected by international guarantees."

The administration was not listening. On July 14 an additional three hundred Special Forces advisors were sent to Vietnam. Two weeks later five thousand more U.S. troops were sent. On August 2, 1964, the White House announced that two American destroyers on patrol in the Gulf of Tonkin had come under attack by North Vietnamese torpedo boats. The Americans returned the fire. Two days later there was another attack. The United States retaliated with air strikes against "oil and naval facilities" in North Vietnam. Shortly thereafter, Congress authorized the president to protect American forces in Vietnam and prevent additional Vietnamese aggression. . . .

In early December, members of the National Committee for a Sane Nuclear Policy (SANE) picketed the White House and called for an immediate negotiated peace. On December 19, three protest groups—the War Resisters League, the Committee for Non-Violent Action, and the Fellowship of Reconciliation—joined their small forces to sponsor a series of antiwar rallies in nine American cities.

These early protest activities, although small, sporadic, and sometimes poorly organized, nevertheless revealed a subtle but continuing New Left shift in emphasis and objectives. Many blacks were tending to resent white participation in the civil rights movement. White activists were shifting from civil rights to antiwar protest.

By mid-1964 the FBI was stepping up the investigation of Communist party influence within the antiwar movement. Hoover later instructed special agents "to intensify through all field offices the instructions to endeavor to penetrate the Students for a Democratic Society so that we will have proper informant coverage similar to what we have in the Ku Klux Klan and the Communist Party itself." Late in 1964, members of the SDS met in New York and decided to commit their resources to a consistent campaign against American involvement in Vietnam. This meeting is considered by many to represent the birth of the antiwar movement. The SDS was more radical in its opposition to the war than other groups. At this meeting members planned a protest march to be held in Washington in the spring. They anticipated, quite wrongly, a small turnout.

EVERYTHING BEGINS TO CHANGE

On February 7, 1965, a small band of well-organized Vietcong guerrillas changed, in one swift surgical stroke, the nature of American involvement in Vietnam—and thus, the course of the domestic antiwar movement in the United States. The Vietcong, operating under cover of darkness, bombarded the American military base at Pleiku with 81-mm mortar rounds. Eight Americans were killed, 126 were wounded, and ten U.S. aircraft were destroyed. In less than a month the United States began a systematic campaign of aerial warfare, called Operation Rolling Thunder.

On February 17, faculty members from a number of New England colleges placed a display ad in the *New York Times* that called for immediate negotiations to end the war. Demonstrations were held in front of the United States mission to the United Nations and on Wall Street.

The U.S. 9th Marine Expeditionary Brigade came ashore on March 8 to guard the American installation at Da Nang, in South Vietnam. It was only a matter of time until American military patrols were engaged in fire fights with the Vietcong.

As the pace of American involvement in Vietnam increased, the American public seemed of two minds. Two-thirds supported the air strikes against North Vietnam. However, the air escalation also revealed that far more Americans were outraged by their government's deeper involvement than anyone imagined. Students and nonstudents alike, many of widely differing political persuasions, were becoming attracted to the ideas of the student New Left and the antiwar movement. The size of the student New Left by the end of March 1965 is indicated by the number of SDS chapters—fifty-two in operation nationwide.

The *New York Times* took notice of the fact that a movement was developing from a quite remarkable patchwork of political action groups. On March 15 the *Times* published its first full-length feature on the New Left with the headline "The New Student Left: Movement Represents Serious Activists in Drive for Change." A number of dissident groups were mentioned, including the SDS, the Student Nonviolent Coordinating Committee, and the Northern Student Movement. The movement was described as "a new, small, loosely bound intelligentsia that calls itself the new student left and that wants to cause fundamental changes in society." According to the article, the New Left's focus of political attention was on "conscription, academic freedom, the war in South Vietnam, disarmament, and poverty."

TEACH-INS BEGIN

Todd Gitlin has written that after the *Times* article student radicalism was "certified as a live national issue." The pace of antiwar protest quickened as SANE sponsored a "March on Washington for Peace and a Negotiated Settlement in Vietnam." Two days later, on March 24, a new form of antiwar protest appeared for the first time in the American political arena: "Teach-Ins."

The first teach-in was organized by faculty members at the University of Michigan to provide lectures, debates, and seminars on American policy in Vietnam. It was an all-night session that attracted the astonishing number of three thousand college students and professors. A thesis of the first teach-in, and those that would follow, was that the Johnson administration, in a hideous distortion of the national interest, was moving the United States in the direction of national catastrophe, possibly nuclear war. President Johnson had misled the people of the United States before the 1964 election by asserting that the Vietnam involvement would not involve American combat troops. The teach-in concept spread rapidly to include more than sixty major colleges. A *Newsweek* editorial said that the teach-in concept represented "a splendid new way of communicating wisdom from scholars, through students, to the benighted general public."

The administration was stunned.

The Johnson administration and the FBI took notice of the teach-ins. Thirteen bureau undercover agents attended one sponsored by the Universities Committee on Problems of War and Peace. Members of the SDS, the Young Socialist Alliance, the W.E.B. Du Bois clubs, and many others were identified by name and political affiliation. Also, the names of twenty-three speakers, including university instructors and members of the clergy, were identified. These data were quickly forwarded to headquarters for review, analysis, and placement in the appropriate FBI counterintelligence files. The first FBI report on this event totaled forty-one pages. Copies were sent to the White House, to the Justice Department's Internal Security and Civil Rights Divisions, and to military intelligence. There seems little doubt that President Johnson read the report. . . .

On March 4, 1965, in testimony before the House Appropriations Committee, J. Edgar Hoover said that the wave of protest against American bombing in Vietnam demonstrated "how unified, organized, and powerful an element the Communist movement is in the United States today." Within days of this testimony, a college professor at an eastern university, doing research on McCarthyism, came under FBI surveillance by the New York field office because he contacted the American Institute of Marxist Studies.

In 1965, the antiwar movement escalated in direct proportion to the escalation of the war itself. Sidney Lens has said that the New Left "movement grew more spontaneously than any leftist force I have ever known, perhaps more so than any in American history."

Hoover ordered intensified infiltration of the SDS in April of 1965 so that [according to a FBI memorandum] the bureau's intelligence division would "have proper coverage similar to what we have on the Communist Party." Large-scale "interviewing"—a traditional FBI method of intimidation—was conducted with as many members from as many SDS chapters as possible. . . .

Hoover and President Johnson met on April 28, 1965. Johnson expressed extraordinary anxiety over the New Left movement and what it was doing to the country. He told Hoover that, according to intelligence reports reaching him, the North Vietnamese and Red Chinese felt that intensified antiwar agitation in the United States would eventually create a traumatic domestic crisis leading to a complete breakdown in law and order. Thus, according to this line of reasoning, U.S. troops would have to be withdrawn from Vietnam in order to restore domestic tranquility. Quite simply, the president felt that the New Left movement was giving encouragement to the enemies of the United States. Hoover advised Johnson that the SDS and accompanying groups were planning to demonstrate against the war in eighty-five U.S. cities between May 3 and May 9, 1965—the largest antiwar demonstration to date. The bureau, Hoover said, would prepare "an overall memorandum on the Vietnam demonstrations and communist influence in the same."

The next day, April 29, Hoover issued instructions for a report to be prepared on "what we know about the Students for a Democratic Society." In the memo he stated, "What I want to get to the president is the background with emphasis upon the communist influence therein." The final report, titled "Communist Activities Relative to United States Policy on Vietnam," proved that the president and the director were completely off the mark. The report said that the Communist Party of the United States (CPUSA) *wanted* to influence antiwar activity but that their influence on the antiwar movement was quite negligible.

A thirty-six-hour marathon teach-in was held at the University of California's Berkeley campus over May 21–22. This event, organized by the Vietnam Day Committee, attracted more than twenty thousand students and professors.

The Nation observed that "few realize just how deeply the teach-ins are reaching into campus life. Trouble is brewing in the most unlikely places."

On June 8, 1965, SANE held an antiwar rally at Madison Square Garden. In July members of Women Strike for Peace, meeting in Indonesia, made the first formal contact between an American antiwar group and representatives of the Democratic Republic of Vietnam and the National Liberation Front. In mid-August the Oakland, California, SDS Chapter, and the Vietnam Day Committee attempted on three separate occasions to block troop transport trains from leaving the Oakland Army Terminal. Later in August the National Coordination Committee to End the War in Vietnam was formed. This umbrella organization of thirty-three different protest groups was the first of several to play a significant role in the movement's nationwide attempt to bring the war to a halt.

On the weekend of October 15–16, a panoply of different groups supporting the movement staged the largest antiwar effort to date. More than a hundred thousand people, in eighty U.S. cities and in several other countries, marched, picketed, and attempted to block troop transports and to occupy induction centers. They provoked furious counterdemonstrations. Many were arrested.

THE FBI'S COUNTERPROGRAM

On November 1, J. Edgar Hoover, speaking in Washington, said that antiwar demonstrators were, for the most part, "halfway citizens who are neither morally, mentally or emotionally mature."

On November 11, the bureau, using the COINTELPRO technique of anonymous mailings, printed copies of an article titled "Rabbi in Vietnam Says Withdrawal Is Not the Answer." They were mailed in plain envelopes to individual members of the Vietnam Day Committee to "convince" the recipients of the correctness of U.S. policy in Vietnam. . . .

Before the end of the year, Attorney General Katzenbach "warned that there were Communists in SDS." Senator John Stennis demanded that the administration uproot the anti-draft movement and "grind it to bits."

A 235-page Senate Internal Subcommittee report was issued by Connecticut Democrat Tom Dodd which said that the anti–Vietnam War movement was, in large measure, "under Communist control."

This type of institutional thinking led to some bizarre activities. For example, on January 22, 1966, more than a year before the official creation of the New Left, COINTELPRO special agents from the Boston field office contacted an editorial cartoonist at an area newspaper. They asked the artist to prepare a cartoon to ridicule a group of antiwar protesters who were traveling to North Vietnam. The cartoon was to "depict (the individuals) as traitors to their country for traveling to Vietnam and making references against the foreign policy of the United States."

In February, the Senate Foreign Relations Committee, chaired by Senator J. William Fulbright, held hearings to review an administration request for $415 million in additional aid for Vietnam. The hearings, which were public, went beyond the aid request to include a televised discussion of the Vietnam involvement. Millions of television viewers discovered that a respectable opinion against the war did exist beyond the protests in the streets. Nevertheless, that month Director Hoover said that the SDS was "one of the most militant organizations" in the country. He added: "Communists are actively promoting and participating in the activities of this organization."

A March 2, 1966, memorandum from the Philadelphia FBI field office reported on an undercover investigation at an area teach-in sponsored by the Universities Committee on Problems of War and Peace, which was attended by antiwar protesters, plus representatives of the Episcopal, Catholic, Methodist, and Unitarian churches. In this action, the bureau was attempting to establish a connection between the antiwar movement and the Communist party.

UNDERCOVER AGENTS AND INFORMANTS

Informants alleged that a Communist Party official had "urged all CP members" in the area to attend. One speaker was identified as a communist, another as a socialist "sympathizer," another as a conscientious objector, and still another according to the bureau had worked to abolish the House Committee on Un-American Activities. This FBI assignment, utilizing the data provided by thirteen informants and sources, resulted in a forty-one-page intelligence report prepared by the Philadelphia field office. The final document was submitted to headquarters in Washington for analysis.

In the late spring of 1966, William Divale, an FBI undercover informant and college student at Pasadena City College, successfully infiltrated the area SDS chapter. At this same time

Gerald Wayne Kirk, also an FBI informant, began his surveillance of the SDS chapter at the University of Chicago. Another FBI informant, Tommy Taft, began to spy for the FBI at Duke University. The student government at Wesleyan College protested the presence of FBI special agents and informants on campus. Their feelings were made known to Hoover, who in a scorching letter of reply said that "Your statements that the FBI investigation is extremely hostile to the goal of academic freedom is not only utterly false but is also so impossible as to cast doubt on the quality of academic reasoning or the motivation behind it." In Hoover's view, the need for additional civilian disturbance intelligence was of paramount concern. Thus, in a letter to the special agents-in-charge at all field offices the director advised, "National, state and local government officials rely on us for information so they can take appropriate action to avert disastrous outbreaks." Field officers "were told to intensify and expand their 'coverage' of demonstrations opposing United States foreign policy in Vietnam.". . .

In October, the FBI made efforts "to discredit and neutralize" a college professor and his association with the Inter-University Committee for Debate on Foreign Policy. FBI headquarters authorized the Detroit field office to send a fictitious-name letter to political figures in Michigan, the media, selected college officials at the University of Michigan, and the college's Board of Regents. The letter accused the instructor of "giving aid and comfort to the event" and asked if his purpose was to "bleed the United States white by prolonging the war in Vietnam."

The San Antonio field office, working with the support of FBI headquarters, attempted to have a Democratic Party fundraising event raided by the Texas Alcoholic Beverage Control Commission. This function was targeted because of two Democratic candidates then running for office. One, a member of the Texas legislature running for reelection, was an active member of the Vietnam Day Committee. The other, campaigning for a seat in Congress, had been visible in his objection to the manufacturing and use of napalm. He had also played a role in sponsoring the National Committee to Abolish the House Committee on Un-American Activities. The FBI saw them as antiwar protesters, and hoped, by publicly embarrassing them, to sabotage their campaigns. In a San Antonio field office memo dated November 14, 1966, it was reported that a prior raid on a local fire department fundraiser had angered the local district attorney. Thus, the Texas Alcoholic Beverage Control Commission decided against the action because of "political ramifications."

By the end of 1966, there had been protests against the war at more than two hundred major universities. Twenty-six percent of all colleges had experienced some form of war protest. More than a dozen "free universities" were established to show "what a radical and non-establishment educational exposure might be." All were operating under intense FBI scrutiny. . . .

By 1967, Lyndon Johnson was reviewing bureau reports on antiwar activists several times a week. He found them to be very disturbing. A White House announcement confirmed that the FBI was "keeping an eye" on antiwar demonstrators for the White House. Secretary of State Dean Rusk said that "antiwar demonstrators were supported by a communist apparatus and were prolonging the war."

The FBI surveillance network was growing more extensive every month. Special agents had no difficulty in working directly with some college administrators. At Brigham Young the president of the university recruited students to monitor the antiwar efforts of several liberal professors. Six were fired. At a number of major universities—Illinois, Indiana, Kansas, Ohio State, Michigan State and Texas among them—administrators worked with the FBI by providing the bureau with the results of on-campus undercover surveillance work of antiwar demonstrations.

By mid-1967, the spectrum of the New Left movement, comprised of hundreds of enormously diverse activist groups, were collectively marshaling their radical energies to end the war. Although most groups had different political agendas, which created internal friction and turmoil within the overall effort, they were somehow able to march together under the New Left banner for the peace cause. The total antiwar effort, however, functioning in large measure without a true national blueprint for action went beyond the vanguard New Left to include a broad spectrum of nonradical citizens from every conceivable walk of American life. Almost one hundred antiwar vigils took place weekly during late 1967. In an effort to reach the nerve center of the war effort, thousands marched on the Pentagon and a few actually forced their way inside but were quickly subdued. Robert Wall, then an FBI special agent, remembers, "When the march on the Pentagon took place in October, the FBI was there en masse, watching, listening, photographing and recording the events of the day." The names of arrested demonstrators were then quickly forwarded to the appropriate FBI field offices. These would become part of the FBI data base in Washington and the appropriate field office. "Hundreds of citizens became the object of FBI surveillance," according to Wall.

In late 1967, Attorney General Ramsey Clark established the Inter Divisional Information Unit of the Justice Department to coordinate and "make use of available intelligence." The IDIU received about 85 percent of its intelligence information from the FBI.

STOP THE DRAFT OR STOP THE PROTEST?

On December 1, 1967, a memorandum from Hoover to twenty-three selected FBI field offices reflected the bureau's increasing uneasiness with the developing antidraft movement. The memo, almost certainly reflecting immense White House pressure, said that "individual cases are being opened regarding leaders of anti-draft organizations and individuals not connected with such organizations but who are actively engaged in counseling, aiding and abetting the anti-draft movement."

Shortly thereafter, thousands of antiwar, antidraft protestors stormed the military induction center in Oakland, California, during "Stop the Draft Week." Other protesters gathered on Boston Common and dramatically burned their draft cards. Dow Chemical, a war materials supplier, became a special antiwar target. Dow recruiters were targeted and harassed during "Dow Days" at Harvard as well as the universities of Illinois, Wisconsin, and Minnesota. On November 15, 1967, another million protesters marched against the war.

In the chronology of the war in Vietnam, the year 1968 was traumatic. The Tet offensive beginning on January 3, a surprise attack by nearly seventy thousand North Vietnamese and Vietcong forces, stunned the American public. Millions came to see that there was no light at the end of the tunnel. The war could not, according to any rational definition of the term, be won. Antiwar violence continued to increase. Ten college campuses were fire-bombed between January and May of 1968. As a means of protest, a million students boycotted classes on April 26. The following day, one hundred thousand marched in New York City. More than 221 demonstrations occurred at 110 colleges between January and June of 1968. An astonishing 3,463 separate acts of campus protest were reported during the same period. Student rebellion was spreading faster than authorities could monitor, intercept, or prevent it. But of all the violence, all the demonstrations, all the chaos and disorder throughout the country, the drama that unfolded at Columbia, a university older than the American republic itself, was the most significant. The events at Columbia, following five years of escalating protests against the war, proved to be the catalyst that led to the FBI authorization for the New Left COINTELPRO.

Exposing the Government's Lies About Vietnam

As the Vietnam War continued amid sustained public protest, the U.S. Department of Defense commissioned a detailed analysis of its own decision-making patterns throughout the war. The study began in the late 1960s and was completed in 1969. This was the most complete history of the Vietnam War to date, and only fifteen copies of the top secret document, later known as "the Pentagon Papers," were initially produced.

During the summer of 1971, it became known that insiders had leaked the Pentagon Papers to editors at the *Washington Post* and the *New York Times*. The U.S. government quickly intervened, using the courts to delay or censor any publication. However, both newspapers managed to publish portions of the study during June 1971. The day before the Supreme Court was to decide whether the newspapers could publish this information, Mike Gravel, a Democratic senator from Alaska, made a last minute stand in favor of the public's right to know the actions of its government. He published the entire contents of the Pentagon Papers through a small press in Boston.

Senator Gravel's introduction to the Pentagon Papers, excerpted below, highlights the information the Papers contained and its importance to the American public. Gravel describes many abuses of government secrecy. Gravel also highlights how many forms of intelligence information, including casualty statistics on both sides of the war, were falsified. The government used this false information to manipulate public opinion.

Mike Gravel, *The Pentagon Papers: The Defense Department History of United States Decisionmaking on Vietnam, Volume I*. Boston: Beacon Press, 1971.

For twenty years this nation has been at war in Indochina [Vietnam]. Tens of thousands of Americans have been killed, half a million have been wounded, a million Asians have died, and millions more have been maimed or have become refugees in their own land. Meanwhile, the greatest representative democracy the world has even seen, the nation of Washington, Jefferson, and Lincoln, has had its nose rubbed in the swamp by petty war lords, jealous generals, black marketeers, and grand-scale dope pushers.

And the war still goes on. People are still dying, arms and legs are being severed, metal is crashing through human bodies, as a direct result of policy decisions conceived in secret and still kept from the American people.

H.G. Wells, the English novelist and historian, once wrote:

The true strength of rulers and empires lies not in armies or emotions, but in the belief of men that they are inflexibly open and truthful and legal. As soon as a government departs from that standard, it ceases to be anything more than "the gang in possession," and its days are numbered.

This is nowhere more true than in the conduct of a representative democracy.

Free and informed public debate is the source of our strength. Remove it and our democratic institutions become a sham. Perceiving this, our forefathers included with our Constitution a Bill of Rights guaranteeing the maximum competition in the marketplace of ideas, and insuring the widest opportunity for the active and full participation of an enlightened electorate.

A VOICE IN GOVERNMENT DECISIONS?

The American people have never agreed that the performance of their elected officials should be immune from public discussion and review. They have never failed to support their government and its policies, once they were convinced of the rightness of those policies. But they should not be expected to offer their support merely on the word of a President and his close advisors. To adopt that position, as many do today, is to demonstrate a basic mistrust in the collective wisdom of the people and a frightening lack of confidence in our form of government.

Our nation was founded at the town meeting, where all citizens had a voice in the decisions of government. Support for policies was insured, for they were made by the people affected. But, with the passage of time, the center of decision-making has escaped the people, and has even moved beyond their representatives in the Congress. With its array of specialists, its technology, and its ability to define state secrets, the Executive has assumed unprecedented power of national decision. The widespread and uncontrolled abuse of secrecy has especially fostered distrust and created division between the government and its people.

We now find policies on the most fundamental of issues, war and peace, adopted without the support or understanding of the people affected by them. As a result of these practices, especially with respect to our involvement in Southeast Asia, our youth has virtually abandoned hope in the ability of their government to represent them, much less to stand for the ideals for which the Republic once stood. The trust between leaders and their people, without which a democracy cannot function, has been dangerously eroded, and we all fear the result.

For it is the leaders who have been found lacking, not the people. It is the leaders who have systematically misled, misunderstood, and, most of all, ignored the people in pursuit of a reckless foreign policy which the people never sanctioned. Separated from the public by a wall of secrecy and by their own desires for power, they failed to heed the voice of the people, who saw instinctively that America's vital interests were not involved in Southeast Asia. Nor could they bring themselves to recognize the knowledge and insight of that large number of private citizens who foresaw the eventual failure of their plans. As we now know, they were able even to ignore the frequently accurate forecasts of the government's own intelligence analysts.

The barriers of secrecy have allowed the national security apparatus to evolve a rigid orthodoxy which excludes those who question the accepted dogma. The result has been a failure to reexamine the postulates underlying our policy, or to give serious attention to alternatives which might avoid the kinds of disastrous choices that have been made in the past decade.

WHAT ARE THE PENTAGON PAPERS?

Nothing in recent history has so served to illuminate the damaging effects of secrecy as has the release of the Pentagon Papers, the Defense Department's history of American decisionmaking on Vietnam. This study is a remarkable work, commissioned by the men who were responsible for our Vietnam planning but who, by 1967, had come to see that our policy was bankrupt. The study was thus a unique attempt, by the Administration that had developed the policy, to look at its foundations and to see what had gone wrong.

A special task force was assembled, composed of outside experts and civilian and military analysts from within the Defense Department. They were given access to all the documentary evidence available to the Pentagon. The result was the most complete study yet performed of the policymaking process that led to our deepening involvement in Vietnam, and the most revealing insight we have had into the functioning of our government's national security apparatus.

We were told that we had to make sacrifices to preserve freedom and liberty in Southeast Asia. We were told that South Vietnam was the victim of aggression, and it was our duty to punish aggression at its source. We were told that we had to fight on the continent of Asia so that we would not have to battle on the shores of America. One can accept these arguments only if he has failed to read the Pentagon Papers.

However, the public has not had access to this study [as of 1971]. Newspapers in possession of the documents . . . published excerpts from them and have prepared their own summary of the study's findings. In doing this, they have performed a valuable public service. But every American is entitled to examine the study in full and to digest for himself the lessons it contains. The people must know the full story of their government's actions over the past twenty years, to ensure that never again will this great nation be led into waging a war through ignorance and deception.

It is for this reason that I determined, when I came into possession of this material, that it must be made available to the American public. For the tragic history it reveals must now be known. The terrible truth is that the Papers do not support our public statements. The Papers do not support our good intentions. The Papers prove that, from the beginning, the war has been an American war, serving only to perpetuate American military power in Asia. Peace has never been on the American agenda for Southeast Asia. Neither we nor the South Vietnamese have been masters of our Southeast Asian policy; we have been its victims, as the leaders of America sought to preserve their reputation for toughness and determination.

No one who reads this study can fail to conclude that, had the true facts been made known earlier, the war would long ago have ended, and the needless deaths of hundreds of thousands of Americans and Vietnamese would have been averted. This is the great lesson of the Pentagon Papers. No greater argument against unchecked secrecy in government can be found in the annals of American history.

THE NEW CULTURE OF NATIONAL SECURITY

The Pentagon Papers tell of the purposeful withholding and distortion of facts. There are no military secrets to be found here, only an appalling litany of faulty premises and questionable objectives, built one upon the other over the course of four administrations, and perpetuated today by a fifth administration.

The Pentagon Papers show that we have created, in the last quarter century, a new culture, a national security culture, protected from the influences of American life by the shield of secrecy. As *New York Times* reporter Neil Sheehan has written,

"To read the Pentagon Papers in their vast detail is to step through the looking glass into a new and different world. This world has a set of values, a dynamic, a language, and a perspective quite distinct from the public world of the ordinary citizen and of the other two branches of the republic—Congress and the judiciary."

The Pentagon Papers reveal the inner workings of a government bureaucracy set up to defend this country, but now out of control, managing an international empire by garrisoning American troops around the world. It created an artificial client state in South Vietnam, lamented its unpopularity among its own people, eventually encouraged the overthrow of that government, and then supported a series of military dictators who served their own ends, and at times our government's ends, but never the cause of their own people.

The Pentagon Papers show that our leaders never understood the human commitments which underlay the nationalist movement in Vietnam, or the degree to which the Vietnamese were willing to sacrifice in what they considered to be a century-long struggle to eliminate colonialism from their land. Like the empires that have gone before us, our government has viewed as legitimate only those regimes which it had established, regardless of the views of those governed. It has viewed the Viet Minh and their successors, the Viet Cong, as insurgents rebelling against a legitimate government, failing to see that their success demonstrated the people's disaffection from the regime we supported. Our leaders lived in an isolated, dehumanized world of "surgical air strikes" and "Viet Cong infrastructure," when the reality was the maiming of women and children and the rise of a popular movement.

POWER IN INFORMATION AND KNOWLEDGE

The Papers show that there was no concern in the decision-making process for the impact of our actions upon the Vietnamese people. American objectives were always to preserve the power and prestige of this country. In the light of the devastation we have brought to that unhappy land, it is hard to be-

lieve that any consideration was given to the costs of our policies that would be borne by the very people we claimed to be
helping.

But the American people too were treated with contempt.
The Pentagon Papers show that the [government's] public
statements of optimism, used to sustain public support for an
increasingly unpopular policy, were contrary to the intelligence
estimates being given our leaders at the time. While we were
led to believe that just a few more soldiers or a few more
bombing runs would turn the tide, the estimates were quite
clear in warning that escalation would bring no significant
change in the war.

The Pentagon Papers show that the enemy knew what we
were not permitted to know. Our leaders sought to keep their
plans from the American people, even as they telegraphed their
intentions to the enemy, as part of a deliberate strategy to cause
him to back down. The elaborate secrecy precautions, the carefully contrived subterfuges, the precisely orchestrated press leaks,
were intended not to deceive "the other side," but to keep the
American public in the dark. Both we and the enemy were
viewed as "audiences" before whom various postures of determination, conciliation, inflexibility, and strength were portrayed.
The American public, which once thought of itself as a central participant in the democratic process, found itself reduced
to the status of an interested, but passive, observer.

The people do not want, nor should they any longer be subjected to, the paternalistic protection of an Executive which
believes that it alone has the right answers. For too long both
the people and Congress have been denied access to the needed
data with which they can judge national policy. For too long
they have been spoon-fed information designed to sustain pre-
determined decisions and denied information which questioned those decisions. For too long they have been forced to
subsist on a diet of half-truths or deliberate deceit, by executives who consider the people and the Congress as adversaries.

But now there is a great awakening in our land. There is a
yearning for peace, and a realization that we need never have

gone to war. There is a yearning for a more free and open society, and the emerging recognition of repression of people's lives, of their right to know, and of their right to determine their nation's future. And there is a yearning for the kind of mutual trust between those who govern and those who are governed that has been so lacking in the past. If ever there was a time for change, it is now. It is in this spirit that I hope the past, as revealed in the Pentagon Papers, will help us make a new beginning, toward that better America which we all seek.

Mike Gravel
U.S. Senator

Washington, D.C.
August 1971

Evaluating the
Antiwar Movement

TODD GITLIN

During the early days of the Vietnam War, Todd Gitlin helped to organize many antiwar protests. However, by the 1970s, he had ended his outright activism to begin his academic career at the University of California, Berkeley, as a sociologist studying the relationships among the media, government, activists, and ordinary citizens, and how they influenced the development of the war. In this selection, Gitlin offers an insider's perspective on the successes and fail ures of the 1960s antiwar movement and analyzes the strategies of both the protesters and politicians of the era. He describes the U.S. government's unresponsive attitude toward protesters as a strategy to minimize the influence of the antiwar movement. However, this strategy was not effective. Indeed, although protesters could not gauge their influence on political decisions and sometimes felt they were accomplishing nothing, political leaders did take public opinion and antiwar feeling into account in their decision making. Gitlin writes that the antiwar movement deterred President Johnson from using nuclear bombs on Hanoi and Haiphong out of fear of a massive American outcry. Similarly, President Nixon decided not to escalate the number of troop deployments in Vietnam in 1969 because of antiwar demonstrations. Gitlin concludes by describing the legacy of the anti–Vietnam War movement for future war protesters.

A s my generation teeters uneasily between late youth and early middle age, and American expeditionary forces are launched toward new wars in the Third World, a good number of my old political buddies are wondering whether the antiwar passions of the 1960s were worth the effort. The Vietnam War dragged on and on, after all, and in the end, didn't Khmer Rouge [the Cambodian government] genocide and Vietnamese authoritarianism discredit our hopes? Prompted by once-over-lightly media treatments of the era, today's campus inactivists also seem to believe that the '60s demonstrated conclusively that you can't change history to match your ideals. So why go to the trouble of letting tainted politics interfere with the rigors of preparing for the law boards?

Meanwhile, it's the so-called conservatives, neo- and paleo-, who give the antiwar movement credit. They firmly believe that the country was seized during the '60s by a "new class" of overeducated left intellectuals, tantrum-throwing students, media liberals, uppity minorities, feminists, hedonists, homosexuals and assorted bleeding hearts, who not only succeeded in trashing tradition, standards, the family and all natural hierarchy, but also broke the back of national security, leveling America's just position in the world and costing us an achievable and noble victory in Vietnam. They have spent the past ten years trying to figure out how to recapture lost terrain from the barbarians. And they are haunted by the specter of revived antiwar activity—for good reason. For despite their paranoid exaggerations and their self-serving refusal to acknowledge just how much ideological ground they have already reconquered, they know in their bones what many veterans of the '60s don't know or have forgotten: that the movement against the Vietnam War was history's most successful movement against a shooting war.

Not that there's much reason for unqualified self-congratulation. The napalm no longer falls on Vietnam, but the country still lives under dictatorship, on a perpetual war footing. Moreover, while the movement counted heavily in American politics, much of the leadership, eventually, wasn't satisfied simply to be against the war. Feeling either futile or giddy, they finally wanted a revolution, and came to define success accordingly. Those who persisted in that course made themselves irrelevant to the politics of the '70s and '80s. If the movement was effective, a less insular and more sophisticated movement might have been all the more so. To understand both the achievement and the limits, to learn lessons apropos impending wars, we have to look carefully at the movement's effects on the war and, with equal care, at the war's effects on the movement.

WHAT HAPPENS WHEN THE PRESENT BECOMES HISTORY?

Already, the passing of time shrouds the '60s; the end is confounded with the beginning, the consequences with the causes; the all-important sequence of events is obscured. Our collective memory, such as it is, rests on a few disjointed images snatched out of order. For example, I was shocked in 1975 when the most sophisticated student in a class I was teaching at the University of California, Santa Cruz, said to me one day, "You were in SDS, right?" Right, I said. "That was the Weathermen, right?" How could I explain easily that the Weathermen were one of the factions that *ended* Students for a Democratic Society, exploded its ten-year history? (As an early leader of SDS I had fervently opposed them, in fact.)

The media and popular lore have dwelt on the lurid, easily pigeonholed images of 1968–71, as if they encompassed and defined the whole of "The '60s" in living color once and for all: the flags of the National Liberation Front of South Vietnam flying at antiwar demonstrations, singled out by TV cameras however outnumbered they were by American flags; window-trashers and rock-throwers, however outnumbered they were by peaceful marchers; the bombings and torchings of ROTC buildings; and the lethal explosions of the Weather Underground townhouse and the University of Wisconsin Army Mathematics Research Center in 1970.

To fathom the antiwar movement, though, we have to go back to 1964–65, when the Johnson administration committed itself to the war. In September 1964, while Lyndon Johnson was campaigning for peace votes with the slogan "We seek no wider war," American gunboats just offshore North Vietnam provoked an attack by the North Vietnamese, and a gullible Senate gave Johnson a carte blanche resolution that was to supply the questionable legal basis for years of subsequent escalation. The political climate of that moment is measured by the fact that the dissenting votes numbered a grand total of two—Wayne Morse and Ernest Gruening. That Christmas, Students for a Democratic Society, with all of a few hundred active members, presumptuously called for a demonstration against the war, to be held in Washington, D.C., in April. In February, Johnson began the systematic bombing of North Vietnam. In March came the first campus teach-ins against the war, and in April more than 25,000 marched in Washington—the majority dressed in jackets, ties, skirts. During the fall of 1965 there were the first coordinated demonstrations across the country, some of them more militant (a few symbolic attempts to block troop trains); there were a few widely publicized draft card burnings and a national media hysteria about a nonexistent SDS plan to disrupt the draft. Within the next 18 months, some leaders of the civil rights movement began denouncing the war—first the militants of the Student Nonviolent Coordinating Committee, then the Reverend Dr. Martin Luther King, Jr. There were attempts to get antiwar measures onto local ballots and to carry the war issue into professional associations.

With the number of American troops steadily swelling to almost the half-million mark and the bombing continuing mercilessly, antiwar militancy—still nonviolent—grew apace. In October 1967 there were vast mobilizations at the Pentagon and in Oakland, California, where, for the first time, armed troops and riot-control police wreaked havoc on active nonviolence. Only in 1968, after the assassinations of Martin Luther King and Robert F. Kennedy, did significant numbers of antiwar people murmur about the need for violence to raise the political cost of the war at home. . . .

WHAT WAS ACCOMPLISHED?

Concrete evidence of the movement's influence was hard to come by. So much so, in fact, that, day to day, many movement people felt we were accomplishing next to nothing. After all, although the worst escalations *might* be averted or postponed at any given moment, this was abstract surmise; concretely, the bombs kept falling, and successive administrations weren't handing out public prizes for tying their hands.

Meanwhile, public opinion after the Tet offensive of early 1968 was ambiguous. It registered the growing conviction that the war was a mistake and a futility, coupled with the desire to "get it all over with" by any means possible, including bombing. This was the combination that Nixon brilliantly exploited to win the presidency in 1968, with vague references to a secret plan to end the war. So emerged the movement's desperate cycle of trying to raise the stakes, double or nothing—more fury and more violence—especially when the media dutifully played their part by amplifying the most flamboyant gestures of antiwar theatre.

Nonetheless, evidence is coming to light that the movement had a direct veto power over war escalations at a number of points. David Halberstam tells us in *The Best and the Brightest*, for example, that in late 1966 the military was already urging President Johnson to bomb Hanoi and Haiphong, to block the harbor and, in Halberstam's words, to "[take] apart the industrial capacity of both cities." "How long [will] it take," Johnson lamented, "[for] five hundred thousand angry Americans to climb that White House wall . . . and lynch their president if he does something like that?" "Which ended for a time," Halberstam writes, "the plan to bomb Hanoi and Haiphong."

Despite their denials at the time, Nixon administration officials were no less sensitive to the actual and potential political threat of movement protest. Early in the first Nixon administration, for example, during a lull in demonstrations—so writes Henry Kissinger in *White House Years*—Secretary of Defense Melvin Laird argued against the secret bombing of Cambodia for fear of "[waking] the dormant beast of public protest." At another point, Kissinger refers to "the hammer of antiwar pressure" as a factor that he and Nixon could never ignore.

HIDDEN RESULTS

The denials were, at times, actually a backhanded index of the movement's real influence. Unberknownst to the movement, its greatest impact was exerted just when it felt most desperate. In the summer of 1969, while withdrawing some ground troops amidst great fanfare, Nixon and Kissinger decided on a "November ultimatum" to Hanoi. Either Hanoi would accommodate to Nixon's bargaining terms by November 1, or Nixon would launch an unprecedented new assault, including, as Seymour Hersh writes in *The Price of Power*, "the massive bombing of Hanoi, Haiphong and other key areas in North Vietnam; the mining of harbors and rivers; the bombing of the dike system; a ground invasion of North Vietnam; the destruction—possibly with nuclear devices—of the main north-south passes along the Ho Chi Minh Trail; and the bombing of North Vietnam's main railroad links with China." For a full month, in utter secrecy, Nixon kept American B-52s on full nuclear alert—the first such alert since the Cuban missile crisis.

Some White House staff members objected to the November ultimatum plans on military grounds, but by Nixon's own account, antiwar demonstrations were central to his decision not to go ahead with this blockbuster escalation. The massive October 15 Moratorium, and the promise of more of the same on November 15, convinced Nixon (as he wrote later) that "after all the protests and the Moratorium, American public opinion would be seriously divided by any military escalation of the war."

For public consumption, Nixon made a show of ignoring the demonstrations and claiming they were of no avail. The movement, for its part, had no way of knowing what catastrophe it was averting, and thus felt helpless. Nixon, meanwhile, moved to split militants from moderates. He combined stepped-up repression, surveillance and press manipulation with a calming strategy that included markedly lower draft calls and, eventually, a draft lottery system that defused opposition by pitting the unlucky few against the lucky. Within the movement, the minority who faulted the Moratorium for its relative moderation began arguing that a new level of militancy was required: first came trashing, then sideline cheerleading for the newly organized splinter group, the Weathermen. The result was a general demoralization on the Left. At the moment of its maximum veto power, much of the movement's hard core fell victim to all-or-nothing thinking. White House secrecy was one reason the movement misunderstood its own force; the intrinsic difficulty of gauging political results was a second; the third was the movement's own bitter-end mentality. Much of the movement succumbed to a politics of rage. Relatively privileged youth had been raised in child-centered families and conditioned by a consumer culture to expect quick results. An excess of impatience made it easy for them to resort to terrorism. Thus, the movement drove itself toward self-isolating militancy and, by 1971, away from most activity altogether. A desperately revolutionary self-image drove the hard core to disdain alliance with moderates, which, of course, was just what the White House wanted.

NIXON'S PLAN FOR PROTEST LEADERS

When Nixon ordered the invasion of Cambodia in the spring of 1970, hundreds of thousands poured into the streets in protest. But the old movement leadership had burned out or burrowed into underground fantasies, and the new activists lacked leadership. This new round of protest flared and disappeared quickly, especially as shrinking draft calls eliminated the immediate threat to many college students. At the same time the killings at Kent State stripped students of their feeling of safety. With their sense of exemption gone, results invisible and leadership lacking, it wasn't long before they subsided into inactivity. And yet, even then, the demonstrations convinced Nixon to limit the invasion's scope and cut it short. "Nixon's decision to limit the Cambodia offensive," Seymour Hersh concludes, "demonstrated anew the ultimate power of the antiwar movement." Even though the frequency and size of demonstrations declined over the next two years, their threat restrained Nixon's hand.

By this time, the movement's influence on the war was mostly indirect: a nudging of the elites whose children were in revolt, which paved the way for Establishment skepticism. Although radicals didn't want to think of themselves as "mere" reformists, they amounted to a small engine that turned the more potent engines that could, in fact, retard the war. The movement continued to stimulate moderate antiwar sentiment in Congress, the media and churches even in later years, when demonstrations had become only a ghostly echo. As early as 1968, political, corporate and media elites grew disillusioned with the war. It wasn't "working." Although they accepted little of the antiwar movement's analysis, the elites capitalized on the movement's initiative and sometimes—as in the case of the [Eugene] McCarthy and [Robert] Kennedy campaigns for the Democratic nomination in 1968—recruited troops as well. . . .

Nevertheless, the war went on for years, leaving hundreds of thousands of corpses as testimony to the movement's failure to achieve the peace it longed for. If it had been more astute, had cultivated more allies, it might have been able to cut the war shorter and reduce the general destruction. The largely middle-class antiwar movement could have broadened in several directions. If it had supported the growing GI antiwar faction more concertedly, had gotten over its squeamishness toward soldiers, the combination might have succeeded in frightening Johnson and Nixon earlier. A more serious alliance with antiwar veterans and working-class draftees might have broken the movement out of its middle-class ghetto, might have established before a hostile public and a cynical administration that the movement was more than a rabble of middle-class kids trying to preserve their privilege of avoiding combat. If the largely white movement had paid more attention to broad-based interracial alliances (as with the 1970 Chicano National Moratorium) and less to the glamour of revolutionary showmanship, it might have capitalized on high-level governmental fears of what Air Force Undersecretary Townsend Hoopes in his memoirs called "the fateful merging of antiwar and racial dissension." As we now know, the White House was terrified of black protest even into the Nixon years. A full year after Martin Luther King was assassinated, J. Edgar Hoover was sending memos on King's sex life to Henry Kissinger, who kept them on file, one National Security Council Staff member said, "to blunt the black antiwar movement."

SHOULD THE NEW LEFT HAVE PUSHED HARDER?

If anything, the movement should be faulted for not being effective, ecumenical, persistent enough. It is even conceivable (history affords no certitudes) that a stronger movement might have kept the ferocious U.S. bombing from driving Cambodian peasants into the arms of the increasingly fanatical Khmer Rouge. All civilized people who are revolted by the Khmer Rouge mass atrocities should also remember that it was the Nixon administration, not the movement, that encouraged the overthrow of Prince Sihanouk and weakened opposition to this regime of mass murders. Moreover, whatever the movement's willingness to overlook authoritarianism in North Vietnam, a shorter, less destructive war might also have made postwar reconciliation easier in a unified Vietnam. And if the movement had survived to demand that the U.S. keep up its end of the 1973 Paris peace agreement, the promised American postwar aid might have overcome some of the austerity that later served Hanoi as a rationale for repression.

The movement left a mixed legacy. Even with most of its force spent, after the McGovern catastrophe of 1972, the phantom movement, coupled with the belated resolve of congressional doves, succeeded in keeping Nixon from a wholehearted new assault on Vietnam. Watergate was the decisive turn, though, that distracted Nixon from keeping his secret promises to Nguyen Van Thieu and short-circuiting the Paris agreements with a resurgence of American bombing. By the cunning of reason, Nixon's paranoia about the antiwar movement, among other bêtes noire, led him to such grossly illegal measures that he was ultimately prevented from continuing the war itself. And, of course, the antiwar feeling outlasted Nixon. As late as 1975, Congress was able to stop American intervention in Angola.

Even today, the memory of the movement against the Vietnam War works against maximum direct military intervention in Central America. Again, there's no cause for pure and simple jubilation: the doves failed to anticipate how easy it would be for later administrations to substitute heavy military aid and troop maneuvers for direct combat forces. The movement also failed to persuade enough of the country that democratic revolutionary change is often the superior alternative to hunger and massacre in the Third World, and that American support (what the New Left used to call "critical support") might soften the most repressive features of revolutionary regimes. The result of simplistic Cold War thinking is hardened revolutions and Third World dependency on the Soviet Union—which after the fact seems to confirm the Cold War notion that revolutions are nothing more than props for Soviet expansion. American troops en masse are not at this moment being sacrificed to unwinnable wars, but the same bitter-end purpose is supporting Somocista guerrillas in Nicaragua, genocidal killers in Guatemala, death squads in El Salvador, a seemingly permanent U.S. base in Honduras—at a relatively cut-rate cost to American society.

THE LEGACY OF THE 1960S

The movement against the Vietnam War can be counted a real if incomplete success, even despite itself. But what happened to the movement in the process?

The movement sloppily squandered much of its moral authority. Too much of the leadership, and some of the rank and file, slid into a romance with the other side. If napalm was evil, then the other side was endowed with nobility. If the American flag was dirty, the NLF flag was clean. If the deluded make-Vietnam-safe-for-democracy barbarism of the war could be glibly equated with the deliberate slaughter of millions in Nazi gas chambers—if the American Christ turned out to look like the Antichrist—then by this cramped, left-wing logic, the Communist Antichrist must really have been Christ. Ironically, some of the movement anticipated the Great Communicator's [President Ronald Reagan] jubilant proclamation that Vietnam was a "noble enterprise," but with the sides reversed. This helped discredit the movement in the eyes of moderate potential supporters—who were, in turn, too quick to find reasons to write it off. For too long the movement swallowed North Vietnamese claims that it had no troops in South Vietnam, even though, by the logic of the movement's argument that Vietnam was one country, artificially kept divided by American intervention, it should not have been surprising that northern troops would be in the south.

Romanticism and rage dictated that North Vietnamese and National Liberation Front heroism be transmuted into the image of a good society that *had* to exist out there somewhere. American activists who thought they were making a revolution, not a mere antiwar movement, borrowed their prepackaged imagery—their slogans and mystique—from Vietnamese cadres whose suffering and courage were undeniable but who had little to teach us about how to conduct a modern democratic society. In 1969, when zealots chanting "Ho, Ho, Ho Chi Minh" confronted other zealots chanting "Mao, Mao, Mao Tse Tung" and tore up SDS between them, both sides were surrendering political reason and curling up to father figures.

MISTAKES OF THE 1960S

This kind of moral corrosion has become all too familiar in the 20th century: the know-it-alls explain away revolutionary abominations, try to corner the market in utopian futures and, in the process, become mirror-images of the absolutist authority they detest. In the end, the revolutionists have helped return moral title to conservatives.

Even today [1983], we hear voices on the left conjuring rationalizations for crimes committed by left-wing guerrillas. A curious partial freedom is parceled out to state-sponsored socialism, as if revolutions are responsible for their accomplishments, while their brutality, if acknowledged at all, is credited to American imperialism. Why is it necessary to keep silent about the shutting down of newspapers in Managaua [Nicaragua], in order to oppose American intervention on behalf of death squads?

There is no simple explanation why much of the antiwar movement leadership found it hard to criticize authoritarian socialism. Partly there was the fear of putting ammunition in the hands of the Right—as though if the Right were right about anything, it might be right about everything. Then, too, dressing up for revolution was easier than reckoning with the strangeness of being a radical movement, based on youth, spunk, marginality and educated arrogance, in a society that not only permitted dissent but made it possible to act in history without wholesale bloodshed. The heavily middle-class revolutionists tried to bull past their own isolation: they made themselves Leninists of the will. Others went the Yippie route, with toy machine guns and glib youth-cult gestures. The publicity loop boosted the most flamboyant leaders into celebrity and helped limit the movement's reach.

WHAT HAPPENED?

Caught in a maelstrom of images, the rest of the movement became massively demoralized by 1970. The vast, unorganized, indeed silent majority was appalled to watch SDS decompose into warring sects speaking in Marxist-Leninist tongues. They didn't think revolutionary Vietnam was the promised land. They hated illegitimate authority in all forms. If they were understandably sentimental about peasants shooting at fighter bombers with rifles from alongside their water buffalo, they also knew that by far the greater bloodbath going on in the world came from American firepower—and that no halfway desirable objective could be worth it. And they were right. From their impulses, on top of the civil rights movement, came a more general refusal of unjust authority, which led, most profoundly, to the movement for the liberation of women. To choose political passivity today on the spurious ground that the antiwar movement of the '60s "failed" is to succumb to all-or-nothing petulance, to insist that history promise to bear out all one's dreams before one tries to stop a slaughter. We'll travel lighter now without the burden of revolutionary myths.

A final legacy of the antiwar movement is that it battered the unreflective anticommunism of the 1950s and made it possible to open new doors. Now it also becomes possible to think past the kneejerk anti-*anti*-communism of the '60s, and to oppose American interventionism on the ground that it violates the elementary rights of human beings, not that it obstructs the Third World's revolutionary emergence into the highest stage of social existence. Anyway, movements are compost for later movements. The Vietnam War bred succeeding wars, and so, in a sense, the meaning depends on what happens as we try to stop sequels in Central America and elsewhere. After throwing weight against a juggernaut once, and slowing it, the right lesson to learn is: Do it better and smarter next time. I like what William Morris wrote: "Men fight and lose the battle, and the thing that they fought for comes about in spite of their defeat, and when it comes, turns out not to be what they meant, and other men have to fight for what they meant under another name."

CHAPTER 4

ISSUES CONFRONTING THE ANTIWAR MOVEMENT

AMERICAN
SOCIAL
MOVEMENTS

A Peaceful Response to September 11, 2001

Writing just before the United States began the 2001 war in Afghanistan, Jim Wallis examines the possible American responses to the terrorist attacks of September 11, 2001. At that time, public opinion was divided along many lines. Politicians and ordinary citizens began to debate plans of action, which included war, foreign aid, and cooperation with many governmental agencies, both American and foreign.

In the following article, Wallis states that the combination of poverty, desperation, and fanatical devotion to religious ideology leads directly to terrorism. Therefore, in order for America to rid the world of terrorism, it must create a peaceful strategy that centers on cooperation, discipline, and patience. Such a strategy must focus on the elimination of what Wallis considers the fundamental causes of terrorism rather than escalate the war. He predicts that further warfare will divide the world and motivate more terrorists to attack America and its allies.

Jim Wallis is the executive director and editor in chief of Sojourners. He is also active in many faith-based efforts to overcome poverty in the United States and worldwide.

L ighting candles at prayer vigils is something many of us have done more times than we can remember. Speaking the language of darkness and light at interfaith services, in liturgical seasons, and in the streets has become a matter of habit. But our darkness feels very real and powerful in this moment—almost impenetrable, and threatening to close in on us.

Jim Wallis, "Hearts and Minds: A Light in the Darkness," *Sojourners*, November/December 2001. Copyright © 2001 by *Sojourners*. (800) 714-7474, www.sojo.net. Reproduced by permission.

And our need for the light feels most urgent.

Old familiar spiritual words must take on a new reality for us now, and a new sense of mission. Words like "Let there be light!" And "A light shines in the darkness, and the darkness has not overcome it." We must not just light candles now; we must make a new commitment.

More than we knew before Sept. 11 [2001], there are many dark places in the world where unspeakable terrorist violence against large numbers of innocent people is being planned. Those places must be exposed to the light of day and the violence be thwarted. There are dark places within us and in our nation that might lash out from our deep woundedness, grief, and anger, carelessly inflicting more pain on innocent people. The light of compassion and reason must prevent us from spreading our pain.

We need the light of courage to face the darkness that lies so thick and heavy before us—courage to heal the darkness in ourselves; courage to reveal the darkness in the very structure of our world; and courage to confront the darkness in the face of evil we saw on Sept. 11. Courage is not the absence of fear, but the resistance to it. In these days, we need to light candles and make commitments so that the darkness will not overcome the light.

Two Paths

Two paths are emerging in response to the terror that has been visited upon us. One speaks the language and spirit of justice and invokes the rule of law in promising to bring the perpetrators of terrorist acts to accountability. Those who so violated the standards of civilized life and the human values we hold most dear must never be allowed to escape judgment and punishment, and the danger of even more terror must be urgently prevented.

The other path uses the language of war and invokes a spirit of retribution and even vengeance, emotions we can all understand. A "war on terrorism" summons up the strength and resolve to stop these horrific acts and prevent their cancerous spread. But the war language fails to provide moral and practical boundaries for that response.

Americans have seldom seen up close or felt the pain that comes from the deliberate destruction of innocent life on such a scale. Until now, it has only been in foreign lands where we have observed the horrible loss that accompanies the massive and violent rending of families and relationships in unspeakable events. Now we understand what many people who inhabit this planet with us have been forced to live with.

"DON'T SPREAD OUR PAIN"

But it is just that collective experience of terrible pain that may now help shape our response. As one woman put it in a radio interview: "Mr. President, don't spread our pain." A rising sentiment in the country wants our nation's response to be born of our best selves, and not our worst impulses. We are hearing more voices asserting that we must not become the evil we loathe in our response to it, and that we should respond out of our deepest values, not the terrorists'.

Our response will become a "test of our national character," according to the statement titled "Deny Them Their Victory," released in September and signed by more than 2,500 religious leaders. It is, indeed, the victory of the terrorists that must now be denied. They and what they represent must be soundly defeated, but the question we face is how to do that. The religious leaders say, "We can deny them their victory by refusing to submit to a world created in their image. . . . We must not allow this terror to drive us away from being the people God has called us to be." They too demand that those "responsible for these utterly evil acts be found and brought to justice," but insist "we must not, out of anger and vengeance, indiscriminately retaliate in ways that bring on even more loss of innocent life."

That conviction is motivated not only by moral considerations but also by pragmatic concerns. America bombing the children of Kabul would create utter glee among the Osama bin Ladens of the world, who would finally be able to raise the armies of terror that they've always dreamed of.

A more courageous response on our part is now required. Discipline, patience, and perseverance in vanquishing the networks, assets, and capabilities of violent terrorists is a path more likely to be effective than merely cathartic. An even more courageous national commitment would be to face honestly the grievances and injustices that breed rage and vengeance and are continually exploited by terrorists to recruit the angry and desperate. The debate about which path to take—justice or vengeance—is taking place in conversations across America, including at the highest levels of political power. And despite American anger at the attacks, there has been significant public opinion opposing indiscriminate military counterstrikes. President Bush's admirable call to respect and protect Arab-Americans and Muslims should help us defend them against reprisals in all our communities, and his distinction between the Afghan people and the Taliban can be invoked to prevent the bombing of Afghanistan.

WHY DID SEPTEMBER 11 HAPPEN?

In addition to the vocation of protecting innocent lives against military retaliation and defending our Arab or Muslim fellow citizens, American religious communities must take on the prophetic role of answering why this happened or, as many have put the question, "Why are so many people angry at us?" The first two tasks, while major undertakings, will be easier to define. It is the third challenge that will require our best discernment and genuine soul-searching.

It is indeed impossible to comprehend adequately the terrorist attack of Sept. 11 without a deeper understanding of the grievances and injustices felt by millions of people around the world. That is a painful subject that the U.S. government refuses to engage, the mainstream media avoids, and many Americans are unable to hear at this moment of mourning, grief, and anger. Indeed, the discussion has the potential to further divide, hurt, and blame ordinary people who already feel very vulnerable and under attack.

People pay tribute to the victims of the September 11, 2001, terrorist attacks at a makeshift memorial in New York City.

But if the conversation can illuminate the confusion many feel, it could actually help in the necessary process of national healing and offer practical guidance for preventing such atrocities in the future. Now is the time to have the courage to face this difficult question. President Abraham Lincoln, unlike most American presidents, pushed the nation to look at its own sins in a time of crisis, to dig deep into our spiritual selves and ask whether we are on God's side, rather than the other way around. We need a Lincolnesque quality of self-examination in this moment. In our task of going to the roots of global terrorism, at least three things are important.

THE PATH TO PEACE AND JUSTICE

First, in the necessary prophetic ministry of telling the truth about American global dominance and its consequences, let us never even come close to implying that America—including the victims of the attacks and their families—deserved that great day of evil as some kind of judgment for our national sins, as the reverends [Jerry] Falwell and [Pat] Robertson have suggested from the Right and some U.S. critics have implied from the Left. In a powerful statement released Sept. 17 by Palestinian poets, writers, intellectuals, and political leaders—who all have deep grievances with American foreign policy in the Middle East—the line was drawn: "No cause, not even a just cause, can make legitimate the killing of innocent civilians, no matter how long the list of accusations and the register of grievances. Terror never paves the way to justice, but leads down a short path to hell." Their statement is called "But then, nothing, nothing justifies terrorism," which serves as a fitting final sentence in any discussion about all the injustice that lies behind terrorist acts. We must draw that same line.

Second, we must not make the mistake of thinking that these terrorists are somehow freedom fighters who went too far. On the contrary, the people that the evidence points to are not out to redress the injustices of the world. Osama bin Laden's network of terror would simply create great new oppressions, as is evidenced in the Taliban, the regime that represents their vision for the future. Their terror is not about correcting the great global gulf between haves and have-nots, about the lack of even-handed Middle East policies, or about the absence of democratic freedoms in corrupt Gulf states.

The terrorists don't want Saudi Arabia to respect human rights, but to be more like the Taliban regime—under which girls can't go to school, acid is thrown on the faces of women without head covers, and any religion or lifestyle different than their fanatical extremism is exterminated. For these terrorists, the only "just" solution for the Middle East and the whole Arab world is to expel all Jews and Christians. And their willingness, even eagerness, to inflict weapons of mass destruction on whole populations is beyond dispute.

The root of the terror attacks is not a yearning for economic justice for the poor and oppressed of the world. It is rather a radical rejection of the values of liberty, equality, democracy, and human rights—and the ambition of a perverted religious fundamentalism for regional and global power. However much the United States has fallen short of its professed values and often contradicted them, this terrorism is an attack on those values themselves; it is not violence in their name or on their behalf.

TERRORISTS ARE NOT FREEDOM FIGHTERS

If we are to tell the truth about America, let us also tell the truth about the terrorists. We are accustomed to thinking in a political and economic framework. This time, we need to shift and understand motivations that are more ideological and theological. The evil of bin Laden and his network of terror may have been foolishly strengthened by the support of the CIA during the Cold War, but this evil is not a creation of American power. Indeed, to suggest, as some on the Left have done, that this terrorism is an "understandable consequence of U.S. imperialism" is a grave mistake of both moral and political analysis. The terror of bin Laden's al Qaeda network is less a reaction to "American Empire" than the radical assertion of an ambitious new empire.

Third, we must carefully distinguish between seeing global injustice as the cause of terrorism and understanding such injustice as the breeding and recruiting ground for terrorism. Grinding and dehumanizing poverty, hopelessness, and desperation clearly fuel the armies of terror, but a more ideological and fanatical agenda is its driving force. Therefore, the call for global justice as a necessary part of any response to terrorism should be seen not as an accommodation, surrender, or even negotiation with the perpetrators of horrific evil. It is rather an attack on their ability to recruit and subvert the wounded and angry for their hideous purposes, as well as being the right thing to do. Evidence shows that when the prospects for peace appeared more hopeful in the Middle East, the ability of terrorist groups operating in the region was greatly diminished. We must speak of the need to drain the swamps of injustice that breed the mosquitoes of terror and find a way to make this a teachable moment rather than merely a blame game.

Despite the famous arrogance of too many American travelers overseas, many people around the world have an affection for the American people while feeling a real antipathy toward the policies of the U.S. government. If ordinary Americans are to find a deeper understanding of "why so many people are angry at us," we will need to overcome our appalling ignorance of world geography and international events and develop a much deeper comprehension of what the American government is doing in our name.

Practically speaking, one idea for our response to the terrorism of Osama bin Laden might be this: Even if the multinational effort now under way limits its campaign, as it should, to successfully rooting out the networks of terrorism and not punishing the people of Afghanistan, that will not be enough.

To be a real international effort against terrorism, it must demonstrate a new compassion, generosity of spirit, and commitment to justice precisely toward those people who have been abandoned and abused. Yes, let us stop bin Laden's plans to hurt more people, but then let us undertake a massive and collective effort to keep the people of Afghanistan from starving this winter. Such a dramatic and public initiative would clearly demonstrate the relationship between halting terrorism and removing injustice. Suffering people everywhere would see the clear signal, and the recruiters of pain would be dealt a death blow.

It's time for justice—for the perpetrators of terror and for the people our global order has, for so long, left out and behind. How we respond to these murderous events will shape our future even more than the terrorists can. As the religious leaders' statement pleads, "Let us make the right choices."

The Antiwar Movement Must Reclaim Its Patriotic Roots

Michael Kazin

Georgetown University history professor Michael Kazin has become a prominent voice for the antiwar movement as it heads into the twenty-first century. Kazin's articles in the *Washington Post*, his commentary on radio and television programs, and his many books have influenced the direction and philosophy of the antiwar movement in confronting the war on terror and the 2003 war in Iraq.

In this selection, written as the U.S. government prepared for the 2003 war in Iraq, Kazin criticizes modern antiwar movement leaders for their failure to uphold traditional American values such as grassroots democracy and individual liberty. He believes that the majority of American people have trouble identifying with the leftist politics of the antiwar movement because of this failure. Kazin provides advice and recommendations to antiwar leaders to ensure they become a powerful force in American politics in the twenty-first century. To do so, they must abandon their cynicism and reclaim a positive belief in American ideals.

As the U.S. military prepares for war, millions of Americans are seeking a way to stop it. Hundreds of thousands of them have attended national demonstrations in Washington and San Francisco. Local protest on campuses, in churches and by labor union members is broader and louder than at any time since the Vietnam War, more than three decades ago. Most Democrats running for president, eager to keep step with the party's base, have warned the White House against rushing into war.

But the American left, the natural vehicle for opponents of imperial overreach, remains a tiny persuasion and a sharply divided one at that. The organizers of the recent Washington and San Francisco marches refuse to say anything critical of [Iraqi dictator] Saddam Hussein; many belong to the Workers World Party, whose stated goal is "solidarity of all the workers and oppressed against this criminal imperialist system." That viewpoint dismays liberals such as philosopher and editor Michael Walzer, who calls for a "decent" left that would never apologize for tyrants. But whatever their views on Iraq, no one in the current peace movement has put forth a moral vision that might unite and sustain it beyond the precipice of war.

Progressives once had such a vision, and they derived it from unimpeachable sources—the Declaration of Independence and the Constitution. They articulated American ideals of social equality, individual liberty and grass-roots democracy, and accused governing elites of betraying them in practice. Through most of U.S. history, this brand of patriotism was indispensable to the cause of social change. It made the protests and rebellions of leftists comprehensible to their fellow citizens and helped inscribe those movements within a common national narrative.

HISTORICAL ROOTS OF PROTEST

Thomas Paine, born in England, praised his adopted homeland as an "asylum for mankind"—which gave him a forum to denounce regressive taxes and propose free public education. Elizabeth Cady Stanton co-authored a "Declaration of Rights of Women" on the centennial of the Declaration of Independence and argued that denying the vote to women was a violation of the 14th Amendment. The Populists vowed to "restore the Government of the Republic to the hands of the 'plain people' with which class it originated" through such methods as an eight-hour day and nationalization of the railroads. In the 1930s, sit-down strikers proudly carried American flags into the auto plants they occupied and announced that they were battling for "industrial democracy." Twenty years later, Martin Luther King Jr. told his fellow bus boycotters, "If we are wrong the Supreme Court of this nation is wrong," and proclaimed that "the great glory of American democracy is the right to protest for right."

One could list analogous statements from pioneering reformers such as Jane Addams [social worker and Nobel Peace Prize winner] and Betty Friedan [author and National Organization for Women cofounder], industrial unionists John L. Lewis and Cesar Chavez, and the gay liberationist Harvey Milk. Without patriotic appeals, the great social movements that weakened inequalities of class, gender and race in the United States—and spread their message around the world—never would have gotten off the ground.

A self-critical sense of patriotism also led activists on the left to oppose their nation's expansionist policies abroad. At the end of the 19th century, anti-imperialists opposed the conquest of the Philippines by invoking the words of Thomas Jefferson and comparing President William McKinley to King George III. Foes of U.S. intervention in World War I demanded to know why Americans should die to defend European monarchs and their colonies in Africa and Asia. When Martin Luther King spoke out against the Vietnam War, he explained simply, "I criticize America because I love her. I want her to stand as a moral example to the world."

It's difficult to think of any American radical or reformer who repudiated the national belief system and still had a major impact on U.S. politics and policy. The movement against the Vietnam War did include activists who preferred the Vietcong flag to the American one and a few star-spangled banners were actually torched. But the antiwar insurgency grew powerful only toward the end of the 1960s, when it drew in people who looked for leadership to such liberal patriots as [Martin Luther] King, [labor organizer] Walter Reuther and [Democratic senator] Eugene McCarthy rather than to [radicals such as] Abbie Hoffman and the Weathermen.

WHOSE PATRIOTISM?

Since then, however, many on the left have viewed national ideals as fatally compromised by the racism of the founders and the jingoism of flag-waving conservatives. Noam Chomsky derisively describes patriotism as the governing elite's way of telling its subjects, "You shut up and be obedient, and I'll relentlessly advance my own interests." Protesters against the International Monetary Fund and World Bank echo [civil rights activist] Malcolm X's description of himself as a "victim of Americanism" who could see no "American dream," only "an American nightmare." For such activists, fierce love for one's identity group whether black, Latino, Asian, Native American, gay or lesbian—often seems morally superior to devotion to a nation that long tolerated that group's exclusion or abuse.

Progressives have certainly had some cause to be wary of those who invoke patriotism. After World War II, "Americanism" seemed to become the property of the American Legion, the House Un-American Activities Committee and the FBI. In the 1960s, liberal presidents bullied their way into Indochina in the name of what Lyndon Johnson called "the principle for which our ancestors fought in the valleys of Pennsylvania." On the contemporary right, popular talk-show hosts routinely equate a principled opposition to war with a "hatred" for America.

Yet the left's cynical attitude toward Americanism has been a terrible mistake. Having abandoned their defense of national ideals, progressives also lost the ability to pose convincing alternatives for the nation as a whole. They could take credit for helping to reduce the sadism of our culture toward homosexuals and racial minorities. But the right set the political agenda, in part because its activists were willing to speak forcefully in the name of American principles that knit together disparate groups such as anti-union businessmen, white evangelicals and Jewish neo-conservatives for mutual ends.

When progressives abandoned that vision at the end of the '60s, they lost something precious and necessary. The left could no longer speak convincingly to individuals and groups who did not share its iconoclastic assumptions. The economic interests of many of those "Middle Americans" whom Richard Nixon and Ronald Reagan lured to the GOP clashed with those of the pro-business right. But the left's grammar of protest, with its emphasis on rights for distinct and separate groups, failed to mobilize an aggrieved majority.

"PEACE IS PATRIOTIC"

On the Mall last month [January 2003], some protesters carried signs that read "Peace Is Patriotic." If the left hopes to become more than an occasional set of demonstrators and grow, once again, into a mass movement, it will have to build on that sentiment and elaborate the wisdom behind it.

Since the attacks of Sept. 11, 2001, the stakes have been raised. Even if war against terrorism and against Iraq doesn't continue to overshadow all other issues, it will inevitably force activists to clarify how they would achieve security, for individuals and the nation. How can one seriously engage in this conversation about protecting America if the nation holds no privileged place in one's heart? Without empathy for one's neighbors, politics becomes a cold, censorious enterprise indeed.

Progressives should again claim, without pretense or apology, an honorable place in the long tradition of those who demanded that American ideals apply to all and opposed the efforts of those, from whatever quarter, who tried to reserve them for privileged groups and ignoble causes. When the attorney general denies the right of counsel to a citizen accused of terrorism or a CEO cooks the books and fires workers who take him to task, they ought to be put on the defensive for acting in un-American ways. A left that scorns the very notion of patriotism is wasting a splendid opportunity to pose a serious alternative to the arrogant, blundering policies of the current administration and its political allies. Now, as throughout its history, the most effective way to love our country is to fight like hell to change it.

The Antiwar
Movement and the
2003 War in Iraq

DAVID CORTRIGHT

In March 2003 the United States and its allies launched an invasion
of Iraq. The U.S. government argued that Iraq's president Saddam
Hussein presented an eminent threat because of strong indications
that his government was developing weapons of mass destruction
and aiding terrorist groups. The United States wanted to remove
him from power, which required war. The United Nations did not
support such a war, and people around the world began to protest,
hoping to stop the war before it started.

As the war began, however, the antiwar movement was in danger
of losing momentum as more and more people agreed with the U.S.
war efforts. In this selection written shortly after the war began,
columnist David Cortright outlines a plan for antiwar activists to gain
strength. He argues that the antiwar movement has achieved many
recent successes and must view this war as a temporary setback in the
long-term goal of achieving a peaceful society. To build support of
the antiwar movement, Cortright presents an alternative to President
George W. Bush's foreign policy. He proposes a plan that favors mul-
tilateralism—the collaboration of many nations to achieve a solution.
He also favors the use of the United Nations to achieve a safer, more
democratic world and to address the threat of terrorism.

Cortright has been active in antiwar movements in the past. From
1977 to 1987, he served as the executive director of the Committee for a Sane Nuclear Policy (SANE), which is the largest U.S. peace
organization. Cortright is currently the president of the Fourth Free-

David Cortright, "What We Do Now: An Agenda for Peace," *The Nation*, April 21, 2003.
Copyright © 2003 by The Nation Magazine/The Nation Company, Inc. Reproduced
by permission.

dom Forum, which seeks nonviolent resolutions to international conflicts.

As the Bush Administration continues its illegal and unjust military invasion of Iraq, we must steel ourselves for the difficult days that lie ahead. We must also recognize that our work for peace has only just begun.

We should not retreat from our core criticisms of Bush's war or be intimidated into silence. This war was and is completely unnecessary. Iraq was being disarmed through peaceful diplomatic means. It made numerous concessions to UN demands and was in the process of destroying missiles and disclosing its weapons activities when the United States attacked. Unprovoked war against another country without the approval of the [UN] Security Council violates the UN Charter and is illegal under US and international law. Such a war can never be just.

NEW CHALLENGES FOR THE ANTIWAR MOVEMENT

The outbreak of war makes our work more important and necessary than ever. It creates enormous new challenges, but it also offers new opportunities. We must organize a broadly based campaign to address the causes and consequences of this war and to prevent such misguided adventures in the future.

We can start by recognizing the tremendous accomplishments of the past few months. We have created the largest, most broadly based peace movement in history—a movement that has engaged millions of people here and around the globe. Never before have US churches, from the Conference of Catholic Bishops to the National Council of Churches, spoken so resolutely against war. Never before have so many US trade unions supported the antiwar movement. In practically every sector of society—business executives, women's groups, environmentalists, artists, musicians, African-Americans, Latinos—a strong antiwar voice has emerged. Antiwar rallies and vigils have occurred in thousands of communities, and many cities have passed antiwar declarations.

The fact that this effort could not prevent war reflects not the weaknesses of our movement but the failures of American democracy and the entrenched power of US militarism. The Bush Administration has shown utter contempt for public opinion at home and abroad. It manipulated legitimate public concerns about terrorism to assert a false connection between Iraq and [terrorist organization] Al Qaeda and refused to tell the American people or Congress how much the invasion and occupation would cost until after the war was already under way.

Our short-term objectives will depend on how the war unfolds, whether it is a short, "successful" military campaign or becomes a drawn-out war of attrition with constant sniper or guerrilla attacks. We hope there will be few casualties, both for Iraqis and Americans, but we know that a quick victory will bolster the very policies we abhor. We urge our government to do everything possible to avoid unnecessary death and destruction. Our short-term political agenda should include the following demands and issues:

WHAT THE ANTIWAR MOVEMENT WANTS

Protect the innocent. The United States should provide massive humanitarian assistance and economic aid for the Iraqi people and other vulnerable populations in the region. We should support the reconstruction and development of Iraq. This assistance should be administered by civilian agencies, not the Pentagon. We should also demand, or if necessary provide, an accurate accounting of the civilian dead.

Support our men and women in the armed forces. We regret that their Commander in Chief has sent them on an ill-advised and unnecessary mission, but we respect and thank them for their service. We urge special support for the families of service members and reservists who have been sent to the Persian Gulf. We call for greater efforts to address the medical problems that will result from service in the gulf. More than 167,000 veterans are currently on disability as a result of their service in the first Gulf War. We condemn the cuts in veterans' benefits approved by the Republican-controlled Congress and call for increased availability of medical care and other benefits for veterans.

Bring home the troops. We urge the withdrawal of American military forces from Iraq as soon as possible. We oppose the creation of any long-term or permanent US military bases in Iraq.

No war or military threats against Iran. We oppose any attempt to coerce or threaten Iran with military attack. It is no secret that extremists in Washington and Israel favor a military strike against Iran as the next phase in the "war on terror." This would be a further catastrophe for the cause of peace and must be vigorously resisted.

No war for oil. We oppose any US effort to seize control of Iraqi oil or to demand a percentage of Iraqi oil revenues. Ownership of Iraqi oil should remain with the Iraqi people. Iraq was the first Arab nation to nationalize its petroleum resources, and it must be allowed to retain control over this wealth to rebuild its economy and society.

Peace in the Middle East. The United States should give active support to a genuine peace process between Israel and the Palestinians. We should pressure both sides to accept a peace settlement that ends the violence and creates two sovereign and viable states.

Support for regional disarmament. The Gulf War cease-fire resolution of 1991 specified that the disarmament of Iraq was to be the first step toward the creation in the Middle East of a "zone free from weapons of mass destruction." The elimination of weapons of mass destruction in Iraq should thus lead to their elimination throughout the region.

THERE ARE ALTERNATIVES

Our response to war and military occupation in Iraq must also include a longer-term vision of an alternative US security policy. The Bush Administration claims that the deadly nexus of terrorism and weapons of mass destruction requires a radical new foreign policy of military pre-emption and the unilateral assertion of American technological power. This is the policy being implemented in Iraq. We must offer an alternative vision, one that takes seriously the terrorism and proliferation threat but that provides a safer, less costly and ultimately more successful strategy for countering these dangers.

The outlines of our alternative strategy are visible in the policy proposals we have suggested in the current debate over Iraq. We support the disarmament of Iraq, North Korea and other nations regarded by the international community as potential proliferators. We favor vigorous UN weapons inspections to verify disarmament. We call on our government to work diplomatically through the UN Security Council. We endorse targeted sanctions (restrictions on the finances and travel of designated elites, and arms embargoes) and other means of containing recalcitrant states. We endorse lifting sanctions and providing incentives as means of inducing compliance. We support the international campaign against terrorism and urge greater cooperative efforts to prosecute and cut off the funding of those responsible for the September 11 attacks.

At the same time, we recognize that disarmament ultimately must be universal. The disarmament of Iraq must be tied to regional disarmament, which in turn must be linked to global disarmament. The double standard of the United States and other nuclear states, in which we propose to keep these deadliest of weapons indefinitely while denying them to the rest of the world, cannot endure. The Nuclear Nonproliferation Treaty of 1968 was based on a bargain—the nuclear powers' agreeing to pursue disarmament in exchange for the rest of the world's renouncing the nuclear option. The longer the United States and its nuclear partners refuse their obligation to disarm, the greater the likelihood that the nonproliferation regime will collapse. The only true security against nuclear dangers is an enforceable ban on *all* nuclear weapons. Chemical and biological weapons are already banned. The far greater danger of nuclear weapons also must be subject to universal prohibition.

THE REGULATION OF FORCE

A global prohibition against all weapons of mass destruction is the best protection against the danger of terrorists' acquiring and using them. In effect, the disarmament obligations being imposed on Iraq must be applied to the entire world. All nuclear, chemical and biological weapons and long-range missiles should be banned everywhere, by all nations. This is the path to a safer and more secure future.

Of course, a ban on weapons of mass destruction would be meaningless without robust means of verifying and enforcing such prohibitions. A world of disarmament will require much stronger mechanisms of monitoring and enforcement than now exist. The policies we have supported for the peaceful disarmament of Iraq—rigorous inspections, targeted sanctions and multilateral coercive diplomacy—can and should be applied universally to rid the world of weapons of mass destruction. The UN weapons-inspection capability should be increased a hundredfold and deployed throughout the world to monitor and verify the universal ban on weapons of mass destruction. Nations that refuse to comply with verified disarmament requirements should be subjected to targeted sanctions and coercive diplomatic pressures from the UN and other regional security organizations. Nations that cooperate with disarmament mandates should receive inducements in the form of economic assistance, trade and technology preferences, and security assurances. These policy tools, combined with a serious commitment to sustainable economic development for developing nations, are viable means for helping to assure international compliance with a global disarmament mandate.

This is not a pacifist vision that eschews all uses of military force. The threat of force is sometimes a necessary component of coercive diplomacy. In some circumstances the actual use of force—ideally in a targeted and narrow fashion, with authorization from the UN Security Council or regional security bodies—may be necessary. In contrast with the policy of the Bush Administration, however, the proposed approach would allow the threat or use of force only as a last resort, when all other peaceful diplomatic means have been exhausted, and only with the explicit authorization of the Security Council or regional security organizations. In no circumstance would the United States or any other nation have the right to mount a military invasion to overthrow another government for the ostensible purpose of achieving disarmament. Rather, the United States would respect the Charter of the UN and would strive to achieve disarmament and settle the differences among nations through peaceful diplomatic means.

Our immediate challenge in implementing these short- and long-term objectives is to change the political direction and leadership of the United States. In the upcoming political debates we must devote our energies to building support for our alternative foreign-policy vision and creating a mass political constituency that can hold candidates accountable to this vision. Our chances of preventing future military disasters depend in the short run on removing the Bush Administration from office and electing a new political leadership dedicated to international cooperation and peace. This is a formidable political challenge. It will be extremely difficult to accomplish by November 2004. We must begin to organize for this challenge now, however, and we must remain committed to this objective into the future, planning now for the additional election cycles that will probably be necessary to realize our goals. We must also recognize the enormity of the challenge we face in diminishing the unelected power of the national security establishment, which functions as a shadow government regardless of who is in office. These great challenges will be met only by a sustained, massive citizens' movement dedicated to the long-term challenge of fundamentally reshaping America's role in the world. The work begins now, as the military invasion of Iraq continues. We have no time to mourn. A lifetime of organizing and education lies ahead.

Cultural Obstacles to the Antiwar Movement

Duane L. Cady

In the following selection, Duane L. Cady identifies what he considers the central problem facing those within the antiwar movement—overcoming cultural and political biases used to justify war. He first presents the philosophical underpinnings of what he refers to as "warism" and "pacifism." Warism, the dominant philosophy of Western culture and politics, is the idea that war is an acceptable method of conflict resolution provided that certain requirements are met. Pacifism, on the other hand, is the belief that war is never acceptable and that, therefore, nonviolent methods must be used to solve conflicts. Cady concludes that warism has permeated Western culture to the point that it has completely eliminated peaceful action as an acceptable answer to conflict.

Cady is a professor of philosophy at Hamline University in Minnesota and is the author of *Humanitarian Intervention and Just War, Nonviolence and Nuclear Deterrence: Philosophers on War and Peace (Ethics, Violence and Peace).*

When you are criticizing the philosophy of an epoch, do not chiefly direct your attention to those intellectual positions which its exponents feel it necessary explicitly to defend. There will be some fundamental assumptions which adherents of all the variant systems within the epoch unconsciously presuppose. Such assumptions appear so obvious that people do not know what they are assuming because no other way of putting things has ever occurred to them.

—Alfred North Whitehead, *Science and the Modern World*

Warism is the view that war is both morally justifiable in principle and often morally justified in fact. While this general view can be expressed in a variety of forms, the basic notion is that war can be morally acceptable and thus that alternatives to war may be entertained only insofar as they promise distinct advantages over war options. Pacifism, on the other hand, is the view that war, by its very nature, is morally wrong and that humans should work for peaceful resolution of conflict. This general view also can be expressed in a variety of forms; here the basic notion is that war is immoral and thus that alternatives to war must be discovered or created and practiced.

Pacifism rarely gets taken seriously in Western culture. Of course there are significant numbers of people who consider themselves to be pacifists, but they are a small minority of citizens in modern nations. The overwhelmingly dominant attitude in the history of Western thought has been to regard pacifism as a well-meaning but naive and misguided outlook; warism—the view that war is morally justifiable—is almost universally accepted. Warism is a primary cultural obstacle to taking pacifism seriously.

FUNDAMENTAL ASSOCIATIONS
In every culture there are fundamental concepts, assumptions, ideas, and values that together form a frame of reference, a conceptual outlook, a world-view or perspective through which members of the culture experience the world. These fundamentals seem so obvious from within that it rarely occurs to members of a given culture that many of the most important ideas of their society are based on foundations that are taken for granted. One example in the Western tradition is the shift in perspective now called the Copernican Revolution. While the way the solar system works did not change, the perception of the workings of the solar system did change as we moved

from an earth-centered model of the relationship between sun and planets to a sun-centered model. This change in basic outlook shook dominant institutions to their foundations. Since we now take the Copernican model for granted, it is hard for us to imagine the basic conceptual shift involved. . . .

Further examples of dominant societal conceptions can be seen in the significance of gender and race in determining economic, social, and educational opportunities in traditional Western culture. Without malicious intent people have taken for granted that women interested in medicine become nurses while men with those interests become doctors; women become secretaries, men become lawyers; and so on. Minority races have been presumed fit only for unskilled labor while whites (white males) aspire to the professions. Here it should be obvious that the unconscious presuppositions about reality can have profound implications for values as well as beliefs. The cultural givens can be like normative lenses through which "reality" is conceived. Only after these lenses are acknowledged and examined can resulting prejudices be exposed. Making explicit the fundamental concepts—the normative lenses—that form the foundation perspectives of a culture is doing philosophy. So is questioning these fundamentals. And so is imagining alternatives. The more basic the hidden concepts, the more difficult is the examination of them.

In contemporary Western culture, warism is a dominant outlook. There is no special burden of moral justification that must be born by the warist; actually, the greater burden of justification rests with anti-warists. This very fact qualifies warism as the sort of unconscious fundamental presupposition to which Whitehead refers in the quotation at the head of this [selection]. It seems so obvious to most of us that war is morally justifiable that we do not realize that we are assuming it; no other way of understanding large-scale human conflict has genuinely occurred to us. As [former University of Alabama philosophy professor] Iredell Jenkins observes, "We appear to act on the assumption that wars are ultimate and ineradicable features of reality, so there are only two things we can do about them: delay their occurrence and make sure we win them when they occur." Jenkins goes on to note that in fact we take war to be such an essential feature of the nature of things that it even seems natural to try to prevent war by threatening it.

The Western inclination to take warism for granted is so pervasive as to form an unexpressed attitude that is manifest in virtually all aspects of the culture from the obvious cases of politics and the popular media to business, education, and even religion. There is no conspiracy needed here; advertising, television, public and parochial school curricula, all tend to reflect the dominant outlook, the fundamental attitudes of the culture. This predisposition pervades culture from popular heroes like Rambo, Dirty Harry, GI Joe, and the Transformers to more esoteric heroes; even the scholar is considered to be the survivor of an academic joust, embattled in verbal attack and rejoinder. The philosopher is a warrior fighting for truth, defending honor and principle, exchanging linguistic blows in a struggle to defeat rivals and win arguments. Virtually across all levels of society we see fights for superiority whenever conflict arises.

The traditional importance of autonomy of the individual, of personal integrity, of rights to privacy, property, and freedom from governmental interference in the lives of individuals, of fighting for what one believes in against all odds—all of these are examples of fundamental Western values that are for the most part uncritically adopted. Warism is another, but it is less noticed, less often acknowledged than these others. In history and government classes students learn about our republic: born in revolution, expanded through numerous battles with native American Indians, solidified in civil war, internationally preeminent after two world wars, a superpower strong in defense of freedom. School curricula offer many opportunities to discuss battles, tactics, heroics, and military leadership; however, one must dig to find mention of advocates of nonviolence, pacifists, models of cooperative rather than domineering domestic and foreign policy. This emphasis should be expected, given the fundamental perspectives that have been taken for granted.

To complicate matters further, Western culture has a tradition of attempting value-free education, placing little emphasis on ethical or political questioning of current or past social policy. Teachers are expected to teach facts and skills; values are to be respected but left to parents, family, and the church. Increased awareness that all teaching is laden with hidden values has tended to make parents and school boards more inclined to restrict materials that are at all controversial, thus avoiding the introduction of values that might be at odds with those traditionally dominant. This tends to reinforce the momentum toward uniformity and underscore *status quo* values. Entrenched in tradition and forming the fundamental perspective by which all judgments are made, the basic conceptions and values of a culture are rarely made explicit and even more rarely questioned from within the culture. When questions are raised, they tend to be met with defensive reactions, thus further underscoring the *status quo* values. . . .

THE BURDEN OF PROOF

Further indication that our common cultural disposition is to consider war as morally justifiable—even morally required—is the fact that pacifists are much more frequently called upon to justify their views than are those who would defend war as a legitimate activity of nations. It is presumed that the burden of proof rests on those individuals morally opposed to war and committed to alternative means of resolving conflict. This is because warism is a cultural given, a national presupposition in the modern West. This is not to say that Western nations are necessarily belligerent; rather, it is to say that the war system, the standard operating procedure of sovereign states constantly preparing for, threatening, and employing military force in domestic and international affairs, goes almost wholly unquestioned. Those at various positions within the political spectrum may disagree about the details of weapons acquisitions budgets, levels of military preparedness, troop deployment, positioning of foreign military bases, and so on, but the system itself is not thereby in question. Given this context, criticism of the war system is typically met with hostility. Political candidates, understanding the dominant attitudes, need to present themselves as "tougher" than the other candidates, need to be wary of being characterized as "soft on the enemy," "weak on defense," "indecisive" with adversaries, or reluctant to "stand firm." All of this contributes to encouraging the dominant attitude and belittling its opposition. The result is that alternatives to the war system—pacifist views in particular—are not seriously considered because "everybody knows" what patently implausible positions these alternatives must be. This conventional wisdom is confirmed through its own media and institutions.

The widespread, unquestioning acceptance of warism and the corresponding reluctance to consider pacifism as a legitimate option make it difficult to propose a genuine consideration of pacifist alternatives. Typically, either it does not occur to the warist to challenge the view that war is morally justified or the warist openly accepts warism. In either case, the conceptual framework of the culture, which takes warism for granted, goes unquestioned. If we assume (without realizing it) that war itself is morally justifiable, our moral considerations of war will be focused on whether a particular war is justified or whether particular acts within a given war are morally acceptable. These are important concerns, but addressing them does not get at the fundamental issue raised by the pacifist: the morality of war as such. In *Just and Unjust Wars* Michael Walzer explains that "war is always judged twice, first with reference to the reasons states have for fighting, secondly with reference to the means they adopt." The pacifist suggestion is that there is a third judgment of war that must be made prior to the other two: might war, by its very nature, be unjust? This issue is considered by Walzer only as an afterthought in an appendix, where it is tossed off as naive. Perhaps Walzer should not be faulted for this omission, since he defines his task as describing the conventional morality of war and, as has been maintained above, the conventional morality does take warism for granted. To this extent Walzer is correct. And this is just the point: our warist conceptual frameworks—our warist normative lenses—

blind us to the root question. The concern of pacifists is to expose the hidden warist bias and not merely describe cultural values. Pacifists seek to examine cultural values and recommend what they ought to be. This is why the pacifist insists on judging war in itself, a judgment more fundamental than the more limited assessments of the morality of a given war or the morality of specific acts within a particular war.

RACISM, SEXISM . . . WARISM

The slow but persistent rise in awareness of racial, ethnic, and gender oppression in our time and the beginning efforts of liberation from within the oppressed groups offer hope that even the most deeply held and least explicitly challenged predispositions of culture might be examined. Such examinations can lead to changes in the lives of the oppressed. Perhaps even those oppressed by warism will one day free themselves from accepting war as an inevitable condition of nature.

Two hundred years ago slavery was a common and well-established social institution in the United States. It had been an ordinary feature of many cultures dating to ancient and perhaps prehistoric times. Slavery was taken for granted as a natural condition for beings who were thought to be inferior to the dominant group. And slavery was considered an essential feature of our nation's economy. Within the past two centuries attitudes toward slavery have changed dramatically. With these fundamental shifts in normative lenses came fundamental shifts in the practice and legality of slavery. These changes have been as difficult as they have been dramatic, for former slaves, for former slaveholders, and for culture at large. While deep racial prejudices persist to this day, slavery is no longer tolerated in modern cultures. Slavery-like conditions of severe economic exploitation of labor have become embarrassments to dominant groups in part because slavery is universally condemned. The point is that the most central values of cultures—thought to be essential to the very survival of the society and allegedly grounded in the natural conditions of creation—*can* change in fundamental ways in relatively short periods of time with profound implications for individuals and societies. John Dewey beautifully links this point to the consideration of warism: "War is as much a social pattern [for us] as was the domestic slavery which the ancients thought to be immutable fact."

The civil rights movement has helped us see that human worth is not determined by a racial hierarchy. Feminism has helped us realize again that dominant attitudes about people may well be values we choose rather than innate and determined features of human nature. It is historically true that men have been more actively violent and have received more training and encouragement in violence than have women. Dominant attitudes of culture have explained this by reference to what is "natural" for males and "natural" for females. By questioning the traditional role models of men and women, all of us become more free to choose the selves we are to be; we need not be defined by hidden presumptions of gender roles.

Parallel to racial and gender liberation movements, pacifism questions taking warism for granted. Pacifists seek an examination of our unquestioned assumption of warism to expose it as racism and sexism have been examined and exposed. Just as opponents of racism and sexism consider the oppression of non-whites and women, respectively, to be wrong and thus to require fundamental changes in society, so opponents of warism—pacifists of various sorts—consider war to be wrong and thus to require fundamental changes in society.

PACIFISM OR PASSIVISM?

Related to the hidden presupposition of warism is a second cultural obstacle to taking pacifism seriously: pacifism is regularly confused with passivism. "Pacifism" (from the Latin *pax, pacis*, peace, originally a compact + *facere*, to make) means, simply, peacemaking or agreement-making. "Passivism" (from the Latin *passivus*, suffering) means being inert or inactive, suffering acceptance. Pacifists may in fact be passivists but they need not be and indeed often are not. Pacifist activists are committed to making peace, making compacts by consensual agreement, contributing to harmonious cooperative social conduct that is orderly by itself from within rather than ordered by the imposition of coercion from without. There is more to pacifism than the moral opposition to war; there is the active effort to understand and make peace. As long as working for cooperative social conduct based on agreement without violence is confused with appeasement and suffering acceptance, there will be no viable alternatives to imposed and coercive social ordering. This confusion of pacifism with passivism accounts for the sometimes hysterical reactions with which pacifists are met when they make their pacifism known. Somehow pacifism has come to mean "giving up, giving in, selling out," descriptions more befitting passivists than pacifists. The truth is that pacifists typically reject passivism. Even [Mahatma] Gandhi, the world's symbol of pacifism in the twentieth century, goes so far as to say that where the only choice is between violence and giving in, he would advise violence. Of course he goes on to say that the choice is virtually never so clear, that nonviolent options once sought can be found. Nevertheless, he states explicitly that pacifism "does not mean meek submission to the will of the evil-doer, but it means pitting one's whole soul against the will of the tyrant." Pacifism is not passivism.

There is less confusion about the meaning of "war." According to its most famous characterization, war is "an act of violence to compel our enemy to do our will" and "there is no logical limit to the application of that force." "War is merely the continuation of policy by other means," composed of primordial violence, hatred, and enmity, the play of chance and reason. In our era, unlimited, primordial violence is called "thermonuclear exchange," and when we think of war we think of tactical and strategic nuclear weapons. Etymologically, "war" (from Old High German *werra*, broil, confusion, strife) means, simply, discord. War has come to mean hostile contention between groups by means of armed force. It is ironic that, culturally, we have lost sight of the positive meaning of peace—that is, concord, harmony—and think of peace as merely the absence of war. Yet it is war—that is, discord, dissonance, hostile contention between groups—that is the negative idea, a breach of agreement, a lack of cooperation, an absence of unity or harmony.

Beyond both cultural predisposition to warism and confusion of pacifism with passivism, a third obstacle to taking pacifism seriously is the widespread inclination to regard anyone sympathetic to peaceful alternatives to war to be a pacifist of the most extreme sort. The common conception is of pacifism as a monolithic, absolutist, religious or mystical conviction—usually arrived at by a conversion experience—that it is wrong always, everywhere, for anyone to use force against another human being. While this absolute position is one version of pacifism, it is not the only one, and it certainly is not the most commonly held version. Characterizing—better, caricaturing—all pacifists as holders of this doctrine polarizes discussion, creates confusion, and provokes defensive reactions. The result is pacifists' being called upon to defend the absolute view when their commitment is to pacifism of another sort. This misconception accounts for the frequent rhetorical question leveled at a pacifist: "You mean I don't have the right to defend myself against an unprovoked attack by a thug in a dark alley?!" (expressed with shock and disbelief). Very often this is raised not as a genuine question but in an effort to attack pacifism, to reduce it to what is popularly thought to be an absurd extreme. This is also attempted by asking, "Don't you believe in a police force?!" (said with a certain horror in the voice), and so on. . . .

OVERCOMING CULTURAL OBSTACLES

These cultural obstacles—the predisposition to warism, the confusion of pacifism with passivism, and the popular caricature of pacifism as a mystical moral fanaticism, unrealistic and naive—all contribute to and help create the hostile context in which pacifism is usually discussed. They come together in a dominant attitude: a good many people take "keeping the peace" to mean preserving the *status quo*. Those holding this concept of peace often enjoy an advantageous position within the *status quo*, that is, they see themselves as well-off in comparison with the social, economic, political, environmental, educational, and physical health of their peers, friends and neighbors, near and distant fellow humans. Any threat to the *status quo*, to the relative advantage, is often seen to require "defense against aggression," often without considering the possibility that the favored status itself may have oppressive implications for others. When some humans enjoy disproportionate advantage, others are subject to disproportionate disadvantage. This is not to suggest that justice requires an egalitarian distribution of benefits and burdens nor is it to deny it. Rather, the suggestion is that the pervasive view of keeping the peace as preserving current conditions, the notion that any threat to the way things are, any change, might "justify" the use of violence, is rooted in deeply entrenched assumptions about peace, war, and the *status quo*. These assumptions are challenged by pacifism. It is not surprising that those who regard peace to be the preservation of the *status quo* are inclined to regard peace advocates with suspicion. Pacifists threaten the *status quo*, especially the pervasive presumption of warism with its implications for the political and economic activities of a society. Emotional, intellectual, and moral strength are especially threatening to those used to dealing in physical strength. It should be no surprise that those who consider peace to be the preservation of the *status quo* are inclined to regard pacifism as incompatible with "the national security" and so on. Perhaps it is natural to see things from one's narrow interest perspective. It is easy to forget that America's eighteenth-century freedom fighters were terrorist guerillas to King George III. . . .

None of us can set aside all our preconceptions at will. But calling the possibility of their being prejudicial to our attention can make us wary and can help us to open our minds, to suspend disbelief, to listen and try to fathom how anyone could take pacifism seriously. It is not easy to make the effort to understand something that is at once respected for its moral strength and disregarded as utopian fantasy.

CHAPTER 5

VOICES FOR PEACE: WORLD PERSPECTIVES

AMERICAN
SOCIAL
MOVEMENTS

The Scope and
Power of
Nonviolence

MAHATMA GANDHI

Best known for leading a peaceful movement to gain India's independence from British colonial rule in 1947, Mahatma Gandhi has greatly influenced the antiwar activists of the twentieth century and beyond, including Martin Luther King Jr. and his struggle to gain civil rights for African Americans.

In this selection written in 1920 at the beginning of India's struggle for independence, Gandhi outlines his belief that nonviolence always offers superior methods of conflict resolution. He establishes that one must always be focused on positive change—the most important concept is to take action for a noble cause. Gandhi even goes so far as to advocate the use of violence when no other options are available. However, he also argues that situations are rarely so simple as to be a choice between violence and submission.

In this age of the rule of brute force, it is almost impossible for anyone to believe that anyone else could possibly reject the law of the final supremacy of brute force. And so I receive anonymous letters advising me that I must not interfere with the progress of non-co-operation even though popular violence may break out. Others come to me and assuming that secretly I must be plotting violence, inquire when the happy moment for declaring open violence will arrive. They assure me that the English will never yield to anything but violence secret or open. Yet others, I am informed, believe that I am the most rascally person living in India because I never give out

Mahatma Gandhi, "The Doctrine of the Sword," *The Essential Writings of Mahatma Gandhi*, edited by Raghavan Iyer. Delhi: Oxford University Press, 1990.

my real intention and that they have not a shadow of a doubt that I believe in violence just as much as most people do.

Such being the hold that the doctrine of the sword has on the majority of mankind, and as success of non-co-operation depends principally on absence of violence during its pendency and as my views in this matter affect the conduct of a large number of people, I am anxious to state them as clearly as possible.

I do believe that where there is only a choice between cowardice and violence I would advise violence. Thus when my eldest son asked me what he should have done, had he been present when I was almost fatally assaulted in 1908, whether he should have run away and seen me killed or whether he should have used his physical force which he could and wanted to use, and defended me, I told him that it was his duty to defend me even by using violence. Hence it was that I took part in the Boer War [in South Africa from 1899 to 1902], the so-called Zulu rebellion and the late War. Hence also do I advocate training in arms for those who believe in the method of violence. I would rather have India resort to arms in order to defend her honour than that she should in a cowardly manner become or remain a helpless witness to her own dishonour.

STRENGTH FOR A BETTER PURPOSE

But I believe that non-violence is infinitely superior to violence, forgiveness is more manly than punishment. *Kshama virasya bhushanam.* 'Forgiveness adorns a soldier.' But abstinence is forgiveness only when there is the power to punish; it is meaningless when it pretends to proceed from a helpless creature. A mouse hardly forgives a cat when it allows itself to be torn to pieces by her. I, therefore, appreciate the sentiment of those who cry out for the condign punishment of General Dyer [a British general known for ruthlessness in India] and his ilk. They would tear him to pieces if they could. But I do not believe India to be helpless. I do not believe myself to be a helpless creature. Only I want to use India's and my strength for a better purpose.

Let me not be misunderstood. Strength does not come from physical capacity. It comes from an indomitable will. An average Zulu is any way more than a match for an average Englishman in bodily capacity. But he flees from an English boy, because he fears the boy's revolver or those who will use it for him. He fears death and is nerveless in spite of his burly figure. We in India may in a moment realize that one hundred thousand Englishmen need not frighten three hundred million human beings. A definite forgiveness would therefore mean a definite recognition of our strength. With enlightened forgiveness must come a mighty wave of strength in us, which would make it impossible for a Dyer and a Frank Johnson to heap affront upon India's devoted head. It matters little to me that for the moment I do not drive my point home. We feel too downtrodden not to be angry and revengeful. But I must not refrain from saying that India can gain more by waiving the right of punishment. We have better work to do, a better mission to deliver to the world.

I am not a visionary. I claim to be a practical idealist. The religion of non-violence is not meant merely for the *rishis* [Hindu gods, sages, and gurus] and saints. It is meant for the common people as well. Non-violence is the law of our species as violence is the law of the brute. The spirit lies dormant in the brute and he knows no law but that of physical might. The dignity of man requires obedience to a higher law—to the strength of the spirit.

THE LAW OF SELF-SACRIFICE

I have therefore ventured to place before India the ancient law of self-sacrifice. For *satyagraha* [nonviolent action] and its offshoots, non-cooperation and civil resistance, are nothing but new names for the law of suffering. The *rishis*, who discovered the law of non-violence in the midst of violence, were greater geniuses than Newton. They were themselves greater warriors than Wellington. Having themselves known the use of arms, they realized their uselessness and taught a weary world that its salvation lay not through violence but through non-violence.

Non-violence in its dynamic condition means conscious suffering. It does not mean meek submission to the will of the evil-doer, but it means the putting of one's whole soul against the will of the tyrant. Working under this law of our being, it is possible for a single individual to defy the whole might of an unjust empire to save his honour, his religion, his soul and lay the foundation for that empire's fall or its regeneration. And so I am not pleading for India to practise non-violence because it is weak. I want her to practise non-violence being conscious of her strength and power. No training in arms is required for realization of her strength. We seem to need it because we seem to think that we are but a lump of flesh. I want India to recognize that she has a soul that cannot perish and that can rise triumphant above every physical weakness and defy the physical combination of a whole world. What is the meaning of Rama [Indian mythological figure], a mere human being, with his host of monkeys, pitting himself against the insolent strength of ten-headed Ravana surrounded in supposed safety by the raging waters on all sides of Lanka? Does it not mean the conquest of physical might by spiritual strength? However, being a practical man, I do not wait till India recognizes the practicability of the spiritual life in the political world. India considers herself to be powerless and paralysed before the machine-guns, the tanks and the aeroplanes of the English. And she takes up non-co-operation out of her weakness. It must still serve the same purpose, namely, bring her delivery from the crushing weight of British injustice if a sufficient number of people practise it.

THE RELIGION OF NON-VIOLENCE

I isolate this non-co-operation from Sinn Feinism [Irish passive resistance to the British including withholding taxes] for, it is so conceived as to be incapable of being offered side by side with violence. But I invite even the school of violence to give this peaceful non-co-operation a trial. It will not fail through its inherent weakness. It may fail because of poverty of response. Then will be the time for real danger. The high-souled men, who are unable to suffer national humiliation any longer, will want to vent their wrath. They will take to violence. So far as I know, they must perish without delivering themselves or their country from the wrong. If India takes up the doctrine of the sword, she may gain momentary victory. Then India will cease to be the pride of my heart. I am wedded to India because I owe my all to her. I believe absolutely that she has a mission for the world. She is not to copy Europe blindly. India's acceptance of the doctrine of the sword will be the hour of my trial. I hope I shall not be found wanting. My religion has no geographical limits. If I have a living faith in it, it will transcend my love for India herself. My life is dedicated to service of India through the religion of non-violence which I believe to be the root of Hinduism.

Meanwhile I urge those who distrust me, not to disturb the even working of the struggle that has just commenced, by inciting to violence in the belief that I want violence. I detest secrecy as a sin. Let them give non-violent non-co-operation a trial and they will find that I had no mental reservation whatsoever.

Only Peaceful Actions Will End Human Suffering

DALAI LAMA

The Dalai Lama is both the head of state for the Tibetan people and their spiritual and religious leader. Tibet is made up primarily of Buddhists who believe that the Dalai Lama is a reincarnation of the Buddha of Compassion. Normally, after more than twenty years of religious and spiritual study, a Dalai Lama assumes leadership of Tibet. However, in 1950, when Chinese forces invaded and took control of Tibet, the fourteenth Dalai Lama was forced into the role of exiled political leader. Living outside of his homeland, the Dalai Lama has made his life into a quest for the peaceful, nonviolent declaration of independence from Chinese control.

In 1989, the Dalai Lama was awarded the Nobel Prize for his work to peacefully return control of Tibet to its native people. In this selection, the Dalai Lama describes the plight of the Tibetan people living under Chinese rule and outlines his conviction regarding nonviolent action for change. He champions his belief that only nonviolent action is appropriate—action that is derived from truth and reason and that will not cause further suffering.

The Dalai Lama has looked to leaders such as Mahatma Gandhi and Martin Luther King Jr. as examples of successful proponents of nonviolence and passive resistance. In turn, the resulting actions and philosophies of the Dalai Lama have influenced modern social activists, including antiwar activists.

Your Majesty, Members of the Nobel Committee, Brothers and Sisters:

I am very happy to be here with you today to receive the Nobel Prize for Peace. I feel honored, humbled and deeply

Dalai Lama, Nobel Peace Prize acceptance speech, Oslo, Norway, December 10, 1989.

moved that you should give this important prize to a simple monk from Tibet. I am no one special. But, I believe the prize is a recognition of the true value of altruism, love, compassion and nonviolence which I try to practice, in accordance with the teachings of the Buddha and the great sages of India and Tibet.

I accept the prize with profound gratitude on behalf of the oppressed everywhere and for all those who struggle for freedom and work for world peace. I accept it as a tribute to the man who founded the modern tradition of non-violent action for change—Mahatma Gandhi—whose life taught and inspired me. And, of course, I accept it on behalf of the six million Tibetan people, my brave countrymen and women inside Tibet, who have suffered and continue to suffer so much. They confront a calculated and systematic strategy aimed at the destruction of their national and cultural identities. The prize reaffirms our conviction that with truth, courage and determination as our weapons, Tibet will be liberated.

WE ARE ALL HUMAN BEINGS

No matter what part of the world we come from, we are all basically the same human beings. We all seek happiness and try to avoid suffering. We have the same basic human needs and concerns. All of us human beings want freedom and the right to determine our own destiny as individuals and as peoples. That is human nature. The great changes that are taking place everywhere in the world, from Eastern Europe to Africa are a clear indication of this.

In China the popular movement for democracy was crushed by brutal force in June this year [1989]. But I do not believe the demonstrations were in vain, because the spirit of freedom was rekindled among the Chinese people and China cannot escape the impact of this spirit of freedom sweeping many parts of the world. The brave students and their supporters showed the Chinese leadership and world the human face of that great nation.

Last week a number of Tibetans were once again sentenced to prison terms of up to nineteen years at a mass show trial, possibly intended to frighten the population before today's event [the prize ceremony]. Their only "crime" was the expression of the widespread desire of Tibetans for the restoration of their beloved country's independence.

VIOLENCE ONLY BRINGS MORE VIOLENCE

The suffering of our people during the past forty years of occupation is well documented. Ours has been a long struggle. We know our cause is just. Because violence can only breed more violence and suffering, our struggle must remain nonviolent and free of hatred. We are trying to end the suffering of our people, not to inflict suffering upon others.

It is with this in mind that I proposed negotiations between Tibet and China on numerous occasions. In 1987, I made specific proposals in a five-point plan for the restoration of peace and human rights in Tibet. This included the conversion of the entire Tibetan plateau into a Zone of Ahimsa, a sanctuary of peace and non-violence where human beings and nature can live in peace and harmony.

Last year [1988], I elaborated on that plan in Strasbourg, at the European Parliament. I believe the ideas I expressed on those occasions are both realistic and reasonable, although they have been criticized by some of my people as being too conciliatory. Unfortunately, China's leaders have not responded positively to the suggestions we have made, which included important concessions. If this continues we will be compelled to reconsider our position.

Any relationship between Tibet and China will have to be based on the principle of equality, respect, trust and mutual benefit. It will also have to be based on the principle which the wise rulers of Tibet and of China laid down in a treaty as early as 823 A.D., carved on the pillar which still stands today in front of the Jo-khang, Tibet's holiest shrine, in Lhasa, that "Tibetans will live happily in the great land of Tibet, and the Chinese will live happily in the great land of China."

As a Buddhist monk, my concern extends to all members of the human family and, indeed, to all sentient beings who suffer. I believe all suffering is caused by ignorance. People inflict pain on others in the selfish pursuit of their happiness or satisfaction. Yet true happiness comes from a sense of inner peace and contentment, which in turn must be achieved through the cultivation of altruism, of love and compassion and elimination of ignorance, selfishness and greed.

The problems we face today, violent conflicts, destruction of nature, poverty, hunger, and so on, are human created problems which can be resolved through human effort, understanding and the development of a sense of brotherhood and sisterhood. We need to cultivate a universal responsibility for one another and the planet we share. Although I have found my own Buddhist religion helpful in generating love and compassion, even for those we consider our enemies, I am convinced that everyone can develop a good heart and a sense of universal responsibility with or without religion.

With the ever-growing impact of science on our lives religion and spirituality have a greater role to play reminding us of our humanity. There is no contradiction between the two. Each gives us valuable insights into the other. Both science and the teachings of the Buddha tell us of the fundamental unity of all things. This understanding is crucial if we are to take positive and decisive action on the pressing global concern with the environment.

I believe all religions pursue the same goals, that of cultivating human goodness and bringing happiness to all human beings. Though the means might appear different the ends are the same.

As we enter the final decade of this century I am optimistic that the ancient values that have sustained mankind are today reaffirming themselves to prepare us for a kinder, happier twenty-first century.

I pray for all of us, oppressor and friend, that together we succeed in building a better world through human understanding and love, and that in doing so we may reduce the pain and suffering of all sentient beings.

Thank you.

Why I Say No to War

POPE JOHN PAUL II

As the leader of the Catholic Church, Pope John Paul II influences millions of people all around the world, including world leaders. When the United States built its case for war against Iraq in early 2003, Pope John Paul joined the antiwar movement and wrote the following article, published worldwide, to explain his beliefs about the war. He outlines the religious and moral basis for his opposition to the war, stating that violent actions are almost never justified. He also believes that the protection of human lives, especially civilian populations, precludes acts of war, even when a war may seem to promise some benefit.

Pope John Paul states the need to pursue peaceful methods, including diplomacy, to promote a peaceful Middle East. He fears that a war against Iraq will plunge the entire region of the Middle East into further desperation, acts of war, and terrorism.

Never as at the beginning of this millennium has humanity felt how precarious is the world which it has shaped. I have been personally struck by the feeling of fear which often dwells in the hearts of our contemporaries.

An insidious terrorism capable of striking at any time and anywhere; the unresolved problem of the Middle East, with the Holy Land and Iraq; the turmoil disrupting South America; the conflicts preventing numerous African countries from focusing on their development; the diseases spreading contagion and death; the grave problem of famine, especially in Africa; irresponsible behaviour contributing to the depletion of the planet's resources; all these are so many plagues threatening the survival of humanity, the peace of individuals, and the security of societies.

Yet everything can change. It depends on each of us. Everyone can develop within himself his potential for faith, for honesty, for respect of others, and for commitment to the service of others.

HUMANITY HAS CHOICES

That is why choices must be made so that humanity can still have a future, and therefore the peoples of the earth and their leaders must sometimes have the courage to say "No".

I say: NO TO WAR! War is not always inevitable. It is always a defeat for humanity.

International law, honest dialogue, solidarity between states, the noble exercise of diplomacy; these are methods worthy of individuals and nations in resolving their differences. I say this as I think of those who still place their trust in nuclear weapons, and as I think of the all too numerous conflicts which continue to hold hostage our brothers and sisters in humanity. Bethlehem reminds us of the unresolved crisis in the Middle East, where two peoples, Israeli and Palestinian, are called to live side by side, equally free and sovereign, in mutual respect.

Faced with the constant degeneration of the crisis in the Middle East, I say to you that the solution will never be imposed by recourse to terrorism or armed conflict, as if military victories could be the solution.

ALL STATES ARE CONNECTED

And what are we to say about the threat of a war which could strike the people of Iraq, the land of the Prophets, a people already sorely tried by more than 12 years of embargo? War is never just another means that one can choose to employ for settling differences between nations.

As the charter of the United Nations Organisation and international law itself remind us, war cannot be decided upon, even when it is a matter of ensuring the common good, except as the very last option and in accordance with very strict conditions, without ignoring the consequences for the civilian population both during and after the military operations.

All states are interconnected both for better and for worse. For this reason, and rightly so, we must be able to distinguish good from evil and call them by their proper names. And history has taught us time and time again that it is when doubt or confusion about what is right and what is wrong prevails that the greatest evils are to be feared.

HONEST LAWS, HONEST PEOPLE

If we are to avoid descending into chaos, it seems to me that two conditions must be met. First, we must rediscover both within states and between states the paramount value of natural law, which was the source of inspiration for the rights of nations and for the first formulations of international law.

Second, we need the persevering work of statesmen who are honest and selfless; in effect, the indispensible professional competence of political leaders has no legitimacy unless it is connected to strong moral convictions.

It will always be possible for a leader who acts in accordance with his convictions to reject situations of injustice or institutional corruption, or to put an end to them. It is precisely in this, I believe, that we rediscover what is today commonly called good governance.

The material and spiritual well-being of humanity, the protection of the freedom and rights of the human person, selfless public service, closeness to concrete conditions: all of these take precedence over every political project and constitute a moral necessity which itself is the best guarantee of peace within nations and peace between nations.

May all of us who have gathered in this place, which is a symbol of spirituality, dialogue and peace, contribute by our daily actions to the advancement of all the peoples of the earth, in justice and harmony, to their progress towards greater happiness and greater justice, far from poverty, violence and threats of war.

CHRONOLOGY

5th century
St. Augustine of Hippo develops the just war doctrine.

17th and 18th centuries
Religious propeace groups begin to organize, citing the contradiction between the wars their kings and political leaders declare and the principles of their religions.

1864
Henry David Thoreau develops the concept of civil disobedience.

1898
The anti-imperialists come to the forefront of American politics.

1917
The Espionage Act provides the U.S. government with its primary tool for eliminating antiwar dissent.

1917
The military draft in the United States is established.

February 13, 1945
Allied forces destroy the German city of Dresden, killing half a million people.

August 6, 1945
The first atomic bomb is dropped over Hiroshima, Japan.

August 9, 1945
The second atomic bomb is dropped over Nagasaki, Japan.

August 15, 1947
India's independence from Great Britain is declared.

June 1950
The Korean War begins.

1956
The FBI initiates COINTELPRO, a program that illegally spies on American citizens. By the 1960s, COINTELPRO focuses almost entirely on antiwar and civil rights activists.

January 1961
In his farewell speech to the nation, President Dwight D. Eisenhower warns against the "military-industrial complex."

October 1962
President John F. Kennedy successfully leads negotiations that halt the Cuban missile crisis, avoiding a possible nuclear war between the United States and the USSR.

August 7, 1964
Congress passes the Gulf of Tonkin Resolution, escalating U.S. involvement in the conflict in Vietnam.

February 1965
The United States begins continuous bombing of North Vietnam.

March 8, 1965
The first U.S. combat troops arrive in Da Nang, South Vietnam. They join twenty-three thousand American military advisers already in South Vietnam.

April 1965
The first mass demonstration against the Vietnam War takes place in Washington, D.C.

June 1967
The protest organization Vietnam Veterans Against the War is formed.

October 1967
Massive demonstrations against the Vietnam War are held across the United States. President Lyndon Johnson's approval rating for his handling of the war drops to 28 percent.

October 15, 1969
National Vietnam Moratorium launches demonstrations and work stoppages across the United States in a national day of antiwar protest.

November 15, 1969
The largest antiwar demonstration to date (attracting some 250,000 people) takes place in Washington, D.C.

May 1970
National Guard troops fire into a crowd of students protesting the Vietnam War at Kent State University in Ohio. Four students are killed.

June 1971
The Pentagon Papers are published, exposing how the U.S. government manipulated information to maintain the Vietnam War.

January 23, 1973
President Richard M. Nixon announces an end to the Vietnam War.

May 1, 1981
Antiwar demonstrators in Washington protest President Ronald Reagan's policies in Central America and his proposed cuts to social spending in favor of increased defense spending.

June 12, 1982
A massive antinuclear demonstration takes place in New York City.

March 23, 1983
In a nationally televised address, President Reagan announces plans to build the Strategic Defense Initiative weapons system, popularly known as "Star Wars."

December 8, 1983
U.S.-Soviet arms control talks in Geneva, Switzerland, end with little accomplished and no date set for future negotiations.

December 8, 1987
U.S president Ronald Reagan and Soviet premier Mikhail Gorbachev sign the intermediate-range nuclear forces (INF) treaty, the first in which the two superpowers commit to dismantling an entire class of missiles.

August 2, 1990
Iraq invades Kuwait. The UN Security Council imposes a trade embargo against Iraq.

January 1991
A U.S.-led coalition launches an air war against Iraq. A ground offensive begins the next month, and Iraqi troops are quickly overwhelmed.

February 26, 1991
Kuwait is liberated.

March 2, 1991
The UN Security Council lays down postwar conditions, including destruction of Iraq's weapons of mass destruction and reparations for Kuwait.

August 20, 1998

President Bill Clinton orders air strikes on sites in Afghanistan and the Sudan, contending that the sites have been linked to alleged terrorist sponsor Osama bin Laden.

December 16, 1998

UN weapons inspectors withdraw from Iraq, which is accused of failing to cooperate with an international attempt to find and destroy its nuclear, chemical, and biological weapons programs. Hours later, four days of U.S. and British air and missile strikes on Baghdad begin.

September 11, 2001

Terrorists hijack four airplanes, crashing two into the World Trade Center in New York City, one into the Pentagon in Washington, D.C., and one into a field in rural Pennsylvania.

October 2001

In retaliation for the September 11 attacks, the United States declares war on the Taliban government of Afghanistan for sheltering terrorist mastermind Osama bin Laden.

November 2001

The last Taliban stronghold falls. Hamid Karzai is sworn in as Afghan interim president

November 8, 2002

The UN Security Council unanimously approves a resolution threatening Iraqi president Saddam Hussein with "serious consequences" if he does not disarm his country.

February 15–16, 2003

Antiwar protesters stage the single largest gathering in world history, primarily using the Internet to bring together 10 million people worldwide to pressure the U.S. government to find a peaceful solution to its conflicts with Iraq.

February 24, 2003

The United States, Britain, and Spain circulate a final UN resolution to authorize war against Iraq, but it does not pass due to opposition from France, Germany, Russia, China, and other countries.

March 17, 2003

In a speech to the nation, President George W. Bush announces the U.S. plans for war in Iraq.

March 19, 2003

The 2003 war against Iraq begins with a missile strike against targets in Baghdad believed to be the command post for Saddam Hussein.

April 5, 2003

American tanks roll through Baghdad, the Iraqi capital.

April 15, 2003

The Pentagon states that the main fighting in Iraq is finished and President Bush declares that "the regime of Saddam Hussein is no more."

April–December 2003

Frequent suicide attacks on U.S. and allied forces claim the lives of hundreds of soldiers, outnumbering those killed during the fighting in March and April.

December 14, 2003

U.S. forces capture deposed Iraqi dictator Saddam Hussein.

FOR FURTHER RESEARCH

Books

Robert L. Beisner, *Twelve Against Empire: The Anti-Imperialists, 1898–1990*. Chicago: University of Chicago Press, 1985.

Duane L. Cady, *From Warism to Pacifism: A Moral Continuum*. Philadelphia: Temple University Press, 1989.

Charles Chatfield, *The American Peace Movement: Ideals and Activism*. New York: Twayne, 1992.

Charles Chatfield and Ruzanna Ilukhina, *Peace/Mir: An Anthology of Historic Alternatives to War*. Syracuse, NY: Syracuse University Press, 1994.

James Kirkpatrick Davis, *Assault on the Left: The FBI and the Sixties Antiwar Movement*. Westport, CT: Praeger, 1997.

Charles DeBennedetti, *Origins of the Modern American Peace Movement, 1915–1929*. Millwood, NY: KTO Press, 1978.

Bob Fitch, *The Whole World's Watching: Peace and Social Justice Movements of the 1960s & 1970s*. Berkeley, CA: Berkeley Art Center Association, 2001.

Robert Higgins, *Plotting Peace: The Owl's Reply to the Hawks and Doves*. London: Brassey's, 1990. Distributed in North America by Macmillan.

Andrew Hunt, *The Turning: A History of Vietnam Veterans Against the War*. New York: New York University Press, 1999.

Martin Luther King Jr., *A Testament of Hope: The Essential Writings of Martin Luther King, Jr.* Ed. James Melvin Washington. San Francisco: Harper & Row, 1986.

Stanley I. Kutler, *Encyclopedia of the Vietnam War*. New York: Charles Scribner's Sons, 1996.

Roger C. Peace, *A Just and Lasting Peace: The U.S. Peace Movement from the Cold War to Desert Storm.* Chicago: Noble Press, 1991.

H.C. Petterson, *Opponents of War: 1917–1918.* Seattle: University of Washington Press, 1968.

Duane Sweeney, ed., *The Peace Catalog.* Seattle: Press for Peace, 1984.

Mark Twain, *Following the Equator and Anti-Imperialist Essays.* New York: Oxford University Press, 1996.

Howard Zinn, *Declarations of Independence: Cross-Examining American Ideology.* New York: HarperCollins, 1990.

———, *A People's History of the United States: 1492– Present.* New York: HarperCollins, 1999.

Websites

AlterNet.org, www.alternet.org. This site features a variety of editorial columns about political and military issues, links to other media sites, and an archive of news related to the 2003 war in Iraq.

Nonviolence.org, www.nonviolence.org. The focus of this site is to promote the analysis of world events from a nonviolent viewpoint.

Not in Our Name, www.notinourname.net. This site offers nonviolent solutions to the terrorist actions of September 11, 2001.

Peaceful Tomorrows, www.peacefultomorrows.org. Peaceful Tomorrows is an advocacy organization founded by family members of the victims of the September 11, 2001, terrorist attacks. Peaceful Tomorrows advocates nonviolent, long-term solutions to the problems of terrorism.

True Majority, www.truemajority.com. True Majority is an online activist organization dedicated to promoting peace, education, and environmental protection.

United for Peace and Justice, www.unitedforpeace.org. United for Peace and Justice is a coalition of more than 650 local and national groups throughout the United States that have joined together to oppose what they see as unjust U.S.-led military actions and imperialist policies.

VoteNoWar.org, www.votenowar.org. This site focuses on carrying out a campaign against war and racism, and supporting grassroots democracy.

Why War?, www.why-war.com. Why War? was formed by a group of students at Swarthmore College to communicate information about the consequences of U.S. military action around the world. The site offers archived links to a wide variety of mainstream and independent media related to warfare.

Win Without War, www.winwithoutwarus.org. Win Without War is an organization devoted to promoting alternatives to warfare.

INDEX

Morse, Wayne, 122
multinational coalitions, 10

Nation (magazine), 104
national security
establishment, 152
natural law, as basis for
international law, 176
New Left movement, 94
Newsweek (magazine), 102
New York Call (newspaper), 66
New York *Herald* (newspaper),
66
New York Herald Tribune, 98
New York Times, 65
on anti–Iraq War movement,
24
first notice of New Left by,
101–102
Ngo Dinh Diem, 87
Ngu, Madame Dinh, 98
Nixon, Richard, 127–28
Nixon administration, 123,
124, 125
No More Parades (Ford), 68
Not in Our Name, 23
Nuclear Nonproliferation
Treaty (1968), 150

O'Hare, Kate Richards, 67
On Civil Disobedience
(Thoreau), 42

pacifism, 154
is confused with passivism,
160–62
overcoming cultural obstacles
to, 162–63
Paine, Thomas, 142
patriotism, Thoreau on duties

of, 47–49
peace, as patriotic, 145
peace movement
vs. antiwar movement, 9
growth of, in U.S., 30–31
precursors of, in Europe,
26–28
Penn, William, 28
Pentagon, 1967 march on, 109,
122
Pentagon Papers, 111, 114–17
Perle, Richard, 11
Philippine Islands
anti-imperialist opposition
to, 143
argument against annexation
of, 34
Philippine War, birth of anti-
imperialist philosophy and,
17
Plymouth (Wisconsin) *Review*
(newspaper), 61
popular culture, encourages
warism, 156
*Port Huron Statement of the
Students for a Democratic
Society,* 95–96
Price of Power, The (Hersh), 124
"Project for Perpetual Peace,"
29
Project for the New American
Century (PNAC), 10–11
propaganda
Cold War, Du Bois on,
71–72
U.S., in support of World
War I, 61
public opinion
Bush administration shows
contempt for, 148

Du Bois on, 73
weapons-inspection
capability of, should be
increased, 151
United States
Du Bois on racism in, 73, 74
early peace movements in,
30–31
during World War I, 56–69
U.S. government
adversarial relationship
between antiwar movement
and, 18
criticism of, is linked with
supporting enemy
in Vietnam War, 104
in World War I, 20
lies about Vietnam by,
exposure of, 111–18
national security
establishment and, 152
U.S. v. Spirit of '76, 67

Vanzetti, Bartolomeo, 69
Vietnam War
exposure of government lies
about, 111–18
M.L. King denounces U.S.
involvement in, 81–93

Waldorf-Astoria Peace
Conference (1949), 70
Wall, Robert, 109
Wallis, Jim, 133
Walzer, Michael, 142, 158
war
confusion in meaning of, 161
economic benefits of, 12

imperialist policies as cause
of, 33–41
political benefits of, 11–12
warism, 153
as dominant societal
conception, 155
vs. pacifism, 154
Watergate, 127
Weathermen, end of SDS and,
121
Wells, H.G., 112
Whitehead, Alfred North, 154,
155
White House Years (Kissinger),
123
Wilson, Woodrow, 19, 58
on need for foreign markets,
59–60
Wolfowitz, Paul, 11
women
first, in House of
Representatives, 67
in peace movement, 31–32
Worcester, Noah, 31
World War I
adversarial relationship
between antiwar movement
and U.S. government
generated by, 18
American protests against,
56–69
anti-Socialist crackdown
following, 68–69
deaths from, 57
of U.S. soldiers, 68
U.S. entry into, 58–59

Zinn, Howard, 56